Science, Grade 5
Table of Contents

W9-CFL-298

Introduction..3
FOSS Correlation......................................3
Overall Assessment..................................4

Unit 1: Physical Science

Background Information..............................7
Unit 1 Assessment...................................13
Matter...15
Properties of Matter................................16
Phases of Matter.....................................17
Molecules in Matter.................................18
Heat..19
Measuring Mass.......................................21
Measuring the Volume of a Solid............22
Measuring Density....................................23
Changes in Matter....................................24
Mixtures..25
Compounds...26
Word Equations..27
Making Carbon Dioxide............................28
How Can You Separate Compounds? 29
Acids and Bases.......................................30
Does the Amount of Matter Change After a Chemical
    Reaction?..31
The Direction of Force 32
Can You Observe the Direction of Opposite Forces? 33
The Force of Gravity.................................34
How Much Force?.....................................35
How Does Force Change Motion? 36
Balanced and Unbalanced Forces 37
Kinds of Energy..38
Where Is the Frame of Reference?..........39
How Do You Measure the Speed of a Marble?.................40
Velocity 41
Inertia...43
How Can You Compare the Inertia of Two Objects?...........44
Accelerometer 46

How Does Mass Affect Acceleration?......47
Static Electricity 48
Circuits 49
Making an Electric Switch........................50
Is It a Conductor or an Insulator? 51
How Can You Make a Series Circuit? 53
How Can You Make a Parallel Circuit? 54
Circuit Diagrams 55
Fuses 56
Making a Magnet 57
Magnetic Force 58
How Can You See the Effect of a Magnetic Field?.............59
How Do Nonmagnetic Materials Affect a Magnet? 60
Electromagnets...61

Unit 2: Earth and Space Science

Background Information..............................62
Unit 2 Assessment...................................69
Inside the Earth 71
Rocks 72
The Soil Under Your Feet.........................73
Layers of Soil...74
Farming the Soil 75
Continental Drift..76
Do the Continents Fit Together?..............77
Boundaries..78
The Plates Move 79
Faults 80
Volcano! 82
Geothermal Energy...................................83
Earth's History..84
Shaping the Earth.....................................85
Erosion..86
Interpreting Map Data 87
The Compass..88
Evaporation and Temperature...................89
Relative Humidity......................................90

What Are the Oceans? 92
Graphing the World's Oceans 93
The Ocean Floor 94
Waves and Currents 95
Observing Currents in an Ocean Model 96
Salty Currents 97
Waves on the Beach 98
What Tide Is It? 99
Lighter Than Water? 101
Earth's Atmosphere 102
The Sun and Weather 103
Air Masses 104
Storm Warning 105
Different Places, Different Weather 106
The Solar System 107
Make a Scale Model of the Planets 108
The Earth Moves 109
Calendar Counting 110
Observing an Earth/Moon Model 111
The Stars Above 112
The Stars Shine 113
Classifying Stars 114
The Universe 115
Telescopes 116

Unit 3: Life Science

Background Information 117
Unit 3 Assessment 123
Cells 125
Plant and Animal Cells 126
How Do Cells Work? 127
Biomes 128
Comparing Biomes 129
Classifying Plants 130
Plant Reproduction 131
Food for Growth 132
Food Chains 133
Backbone or No Backbone 134

Kinds of Animals 135
Life Cycles 136
Reptiles and Birds 137
Birds 138
Mammals 139
The Web of Life 140
Decomposers 141
Plants and Animals Adapt 143
People and the Environment 144
Pollution 145
We're Organized 147
Systems Working Together 148
The Digestive System 149
The Small Intestine 150
The Circulatory System 151
Follow That Blood! 152
Blood Cells 153
The Respiratory System 154
Respiration Rates 155
The Skeletal System 156
The Muscular System 157
How Is Your Muscle Tone? 158
Reproduction and Heredity 159
Sense Organs and the Brain 161
Your Sense of Smell 162
Your Sense of Taste 163
Test Your Sense of Taste 164
Your Sense of Hearing 165
Are Two Ears Better Than One? 166
Your Sense of Sight 167
How Does Light Affect the Pupils of Your Eyes? 168
Seeing an Afterimage 169
Your Sense of Touch 170
How Does Skin Protect Against Infection? 171
Good Hygiene 172

Answer Key 173

Introduction

Children see the world around them and ask questions that naturally lead into the lessons that they will be taught in science. Science is exciting to children because it answers their questions about themselves and the world around them—their immediate world and their larger environment. They should be encouraged to observe their world, the things in it, and how things interact. A basic understanding of science boosts students' understanding of the world around them.

Organization

Science provides information on a variety of basic science concepts. It is broken into three units: Physical Science, Earth and Space Science, and Life Science. Each unit contains concise background information on the unit's topics, as well as exercises and activities to reinforce students' knowledge and understanding of basic principles of science and the world around them.

This book contains three types of pages:
- Concise background information is provided for each unit. These pages are intended for the teacher's use or for helpers to read to the class.

- Assessments are included for use as tests or practice for the students. These pages are meant to be reproduced.

- Activity pages contain information on a subject, or they list the materials and steps necessary for students to complete a project. Questions for students to answer are also included on these pages as a type of performance assessment. As much as possible, these activities include most of the multiple intelligences so students can use their strengths to achieve a well-balanced learning style. These pages are also meant for reproduction for use by students.

Use

Science is designed for independent use by students who have been introduced to the skills and concepts described. Copies of the activities can be given to individuals, pairs of students, or small groups for completion. They may also be used as a center activity. If students are familiar with the content, the worksheets may also be used as homework.

Hands-On Experience

An understanding of science is best promoted by hands-on experience. *Science* provides a wide variety of activities for students to do. But students also need real-life exposure to their world. Playgrounds, parks, and vacant lots are handy study sites to observe many of nature's forces and changes.

It is essential that students be given sufficient concrete examples of scientific concepts. Appropriate manipulatives can be bought or made from common everyday objects. Most of the activity pages can be completed with materials easily accessible to the students.

Suggestions for Use

- **Bulletin Board:** Display completed work to show student progress.

- **Portfolios:** Have your students maintain a portfolio of their completed exercises and activities or of newspaper articles about current events in science. This portfolio can help you in performance assessment.

- **Assessments:** Use the overall and unit assessments as diagnostic tools by administering them before students begin the activities. After students have completed each unit, let them retake the unit test to see the progress they have made.

- **Center Activities:** Use the worksheets as a center activity to give students the opportunity to work cooperatively.

- **Fun:** Have fun with these activities while you and your students uncover the basic principles of science.

FOSS Correlation

The Full Option Science System™ (FOSS) was developed at the University of California at Berkeley. It is a coordinated science curriculum organized into four categories: Life Science; Physical Science; Earth Science; and Scientific Reasoning and Technology. Under each category are various modules that span two grade levels. The modules for this grade level are highlighted below.

Physical Science
- Levers and Pulleys: See *Science*, grade 3, *Science*, grade 4, and *Science*, grade 6, in this series.
- Mixtures and Solutions: 25–31; Also, see *Science*, grade 3, and *Science*, grade 6, in this series.

Earth Science
- Solar Energy: 103–106; Also, see *Science*, grade 6, in this series.
- Landforms: 71–87, 92–98; Also, see *Science*, grade 6, in this series.

Life Science
- Food and Nutrition: See *Science*, grade 6, in this series.
- Environments: 128–146; Also, see *Science*, grade 6, in this series.

Overall Assessment

📦 **Read each statement. Write _T_ on the line if the statement is true. Write _F_ if the statement is false.**

_____ 1. Matter can be described by properties of color and taste.

_____ 2. Cutting paper is an example of a physical change.

_____ 3. Friction is a force that resists movement.

_____ 4. Speed is calculated by multiplying the distance traveled by the travel time.

_____ 5. Current flows easily through an insulator.

_____ 6. The like poles of two different magnets will repel each other.

📦 **Darken the letter of the best answer.**

7. Water can change into a gas through _____.
   - Ⓐ condensation
   - Ⓑ evaporation
   - Ⓒ chemical change
   - Ⓓ cooling

8. Water is _____.
   - Ⓐ an element
   - Ⓑ a compound
   - Ⓒ a solution
   - Ⓓ an atom

9. The force that pulls things toward each other is called _____.
   - Ⓐ friction
   - Ⓑ mass
   - Ⓒ motion
   - Ⓓ gravity

10. In what way is friction useful to a skydiver?
   - Ⓐ It speeds up the fall.
   - Ⓑ It slows down the fall.
   - Ⓒ It holds air in the parachute.
   - Ⓓ It increases the pull of gravity.

11. The ends of a magnet are called _____.
   - Ⓐ the poles
   - Ⓑ the lines of force
   - Ⓒ a magnetic field
   - Ⓓ a magnetic force

12. If one of the lights goes out in a series circuit, the others will _____.
   - Ⓐ go out
   - Ⓑ become brighter
   - Ⓒ become dimmer
   - Ⓓ remain the same

GO ON TO THE NEXT PAGE ☞👆

Overall Assessment, p. 2

Read each statement. Write *T* on the line if the statement is true. Write *F* if the statement is false.

_____ **13.** The top layer of the Earth is called the crust.

_____ **14.** A fault is a crack in the Earth's crust.

_____ **15.** Soil is created through a very long process.

_____ **16.** An area's climate is its average weather over a long period of time.

_____ **17.** Oceans cover over two thirds of the Earth's surface.

_____ **18.** Tides are caused by the Moon's gravitational pull.

Darken the letter of the answer that best completes each sentence.

19. The three main kinds of rocks are _____.
Ⓐ hard, soft, and medium
Ⓑ igneous, sedimentary, and metamorphic
Ⓒ troposphere, stratosphere, and ionosphere
Ⓓ glaciers, mountains, and volcanoes

20. Erosion occurs when _____.
Ⓐ soil is added to the ground
Ⓑ dams are built
Ⓒ rocks and soil are carried away by wind and water
Ⓓ grass and trees are planted

21. Soil is made up of _____.
Ⓐ cardboard and paper
Ⓑ water and snow
Ⓒ rock, organic materials, water, and air
Ⓓ sunlight and rain

22. Humidity is the amount of _____.
Ⓐ oxygen in the air
Ⓑ water vapor in the air
Ⓒ dust in the air
Ⓓ rain that falls

23. Clouds, rain, air temperature, and wind are all part of the Earth's _____.
Ⓐ core
Ⓑ plates
Ⓒ ionsphere
Ⓓ weather

24. A group of billions of stars is called a _____.
Ⓐ galaxy
Ⓑ solar system
Ⓒ constellation
Ⓓ meteor shower

GO ON TO THE NEXT PAGE ☞

Overall Assessment, p. 3

Match the terms at the right with the definitions at the left. Write the letter of the correct term on the line.

_____ **25.** one of the major theories of life science

_____ **26.** the movement of a material into an area that has less of the material

_____ **27.** loss of water

_____ **28.** organelles that make food in plant cells

_____ **29.** the living material between a cell's nucleus and its cell membrane

_____ **30.** the basic unit of structure and function in an organism

a. cell

b. cell theory

c. chloroplasts

d. cytoplasm

e. dehydration

f. diffusion

Use words from the box to complete the sentences.

vertebrates	amphibians	carbon dioxide
mammals	photosynthesis	gymnosperms

31. Plants take in _____.

32. Animals that live part of their lives in water and part on land are called

_____.

33. Animals with backbones are called _____.

34. _____ is the process by which plants make food.

35. Animals with hair or fur are called _____.

36. Plants that reproduce by seeds in cones are _____.

Unit 1: Physical Science

BACKGROUND INFORMATION

Matter

Matter is all around. It is everything that we see and touch. Matter has mass, or weight, and takes up space. Matter is identified in three forms: solid, liquid, and gas. Matter can be easily described by its properties, both physical and chemical. Physical properties describe how a substance looks, which includes color, shape, texture, melting point, and boiling point. Chemical properties tell how something reacts with another substance so that it changes in its appearance, taste, or smell. For example, iron reacts with oxygen and water to make a new substance, rust.

All matter is made up of tiny particles called molecules. Molecules are made up of even smaller particles called atoms. Molecules cannot be seen with a microscope, but students can understand a substance's properties by using their senses when performing simple experiments. For example, if sugar is dissolved in water, the sugar cannot be seen; but it can be detected through taste because the water is sweet.

Solids, Liquids, and Gases

The state of matter is determined by the density of the molecules and how fast they move. In a solid, the molecules are attracted to each other and are tightly held together. The movement of the particles is limited; they vibrate only. Therefore, a solid has a definite shape and volume. A solid's mass is measured in grams (g), a metric weight which is a scientific measurement standard.

Liquids have a definite volume, but they take the shape of the container. The molecules in a liquid are not packed as tightly, so they can move about more freely and easily by sliding over each other. This movement is what makes a liquid take the shape of the

container. The volume of a liquid is measured in milliliters (mL), the scientific standard measurement for liquid.

Gas is the third state of matter. In a gas, the molecules are far apart and move very quickly and randomly in all directions. They bounce off each other when they collide. Gas has no definite shape or volume. Gas, therefore, expands to take the shape of a container. Gas is also measured in milliliters (mL).

Changes in Matter

All matter can change form, meaning it can change from one state to another. When matter changes, nothing is lost or gained; the molecules stay the same. The addition or the removal of heat causes the molecules to get closer or farther apart. The greater the amount of heat, the faster the molecules move. These changes in the density and the speed of a substance's molecules cause the state of matter to change.

When a solid is heated, the molecules expand. They vibrate faster and slip out of position, resulting in the solid changing into a liquid. This process is called melting, and the point at which the solid changes to a liquid is called the melting point. All matter, including rocks, has a melting point. The most commonly recognized melting point (or freezing point) is that of water, which is 0° on the Celsius scale or 32° on the Fahrenheit scale. Even with this change, the structure of the molecules stays the same.

When liquid is heated, the loose molecules continue to expand. The vibration increases, causing them to collide with each other and move in all directions. When the boiling point is reached, the liquid changes into a gas. The most commonly recognized boiling point is that of water. It boils at 100° Celsius or 212° Fahrenheit. This process is called evaporation. Again, the molecules stay the same; nothing is lost or gained when the matter changes states.

The removal of heat causes the reverse changes in matter. Through condensation, a gas is cooled, and the molecules contract. They stop colliding and return to their loosely packed state, thus becoming a liquid. If heat is removed to the point that a liquid reaches its freezing point, a liquid will become a solid. The molecules are densely packed and cannot slide around. In any of these changes, nothing is lost or gained; only the properties of matter change.

Physical Changes

Matter can be changed in two ways, either in a physical change or in a chemical change. A physical change in matter is a change in which the molecules of a substance or substances do not change. There are three kinds of physical change. When matter changes states, as explained above, it is one kind of physical change. A second kind of physical change takes place when a mixture is made. A mixture is a combination of substances in which the molecules of the substances diffuse evenly. Each substance retains its own properties and can be detected by the senses. A third kind of physical change takes place when the shape of a substance is changed through cutting, ripping, or grinding. A log can be cut into many pieces. What remains are sawdust and cut logs. The molecules of the log itself have not changed.

Chemical Changes

When the molecules of a substance change and it exhibits new properties, a chemical change has taken place. A new substance is always made in a chemical change, but molecules are never lost. Even though new molecules are made, the same number of atoms exists. Energy, generally in the form of heat, causes the atoms in molecules to form different molecules. Baking is a common example of a chemical change. Sugar, milk, eggs, and flour are combined to make a cake batter mixture. When heat is added, a chemical change takes place to turn the ingredients into a cake. Chemical

changes also occur in the human body. Through chemical changes, food and oxygen react in the body's cells to create energy to make the body work.

When two or more elements combine in a chemical change, a compound forms. For example, two hydrogen atoms and one oxygen atom make water. A model can be drawn to show the makeup. Chemistry uses letter symbols for elements. The formula for water is H_2O. It shows the number of atoms and the elements in it:

$$2 \text{ hydrogen} + 1 \text{ oxygen} \longrightarrow \text{water}$$

Acids and Bases

Compounds can be divided into categories of acids, bases, and neutrals. Acids have a bitter or sour taste, whereas bases have a soapy feel. Lemon juice, carbonated drinks, and vinegar are examples of acids. Soap and ammonia are bases.

Litmus paper or pH paper is used to determine the classification of a substance. With blue litmus paper, an acid will change the paper to pink. With pink litmus, however, an acid will not change its color. The reverse is true for a base. A base will turn pink litmus to blue, while not affecting the color of blue litmus paper. A neutral substance will not change the color of either paper.

Force

A force is simply a push or a pull. Forces can be balanced or unbalanced, and the interactions of these kinds of forces create motion. If forces are balanced, there is no movement. Forces also differ in size and direction. To move a book, it takes a small amount of force; but to move a bookshelf, it would take much more force. Forces can come from up, down, left, and right.

Forces are measured in newtons. They can be added and subtracted. If forces are going in the same direction, they are added. For example, if someone is pushing a wagon and another person is pulling the wagon, the amounts of force being exerted can be added together. However, if people are pulling in opposite directions, as in a tug-of-war, the forces would be subtracted. The team having the greater number of newtons would have a greater force and would win.

Friction

Friction is a force that keeps resting objects from moving and tends to slow motion when one object rubs against another object. Every motion is affected by friction. An object's surface determines the amount of friction. Rough surfaces create more friction. Smooth surfaces have less friction, so motion is easier. Mass and surface areas of objects also affect the amount of friction. The heavier an object is, the greater the amount of friction. Similarly, when large surface areas come into contact during motion, friction is greater. By reducing the contact of the surface areas, the object can be moved more easily. In some cases, friction can be reduced by using lubricants, materials like oil or soap. Lubricants coat the surface of an object to decrease rubbing.

Gravity

Gravity is a force that attracts all objects that have mass. It is the force that keeps all objects from flying off the surface of the Earth. It is also the force that keeps the planets, Moon, and stars in orbit. Everything on Earth is pulled to the center of the Earth by this unseen force. Sir Isaac Newton called this force gravitation. The more massive an object, the greater the gravitational force that will be exerted. On Earth, the force of gravitation is about 9.8 newtons per kilometer.

A concept that is difficult for students to understand is the difference in the terms *mass* and *weight*. Mass is the measure of the amount of matter in an object. Mass is measured in grams (g). Weight is the measure of the force of gravity on an object. A spring scale measures weight using newtons. When students step on a scale, they are actually measuring their mass, since weight is measured in newtons. It can best be explained by comparing the mass and weight of a person on Earth and on the Moon. The mass of the person stays the same in either place. However, the weight of the person on the Moon will be one sixth of the weight on Earth. The gravitational pull is one sixth less on the Moon since the Moon has less mass.

Inertia

Inertia is the tendency for all objects to stay still or to keep moving if they are moving. This concept is known as the *first law of motion*, or the *law of inertia*, and was explained by Sir Issac Newton in the 1700s. Inertia is a property of mass. The more mass an object has, the more it resists a change in its state. Likewise, the greater the mass, the greater the inertia. Once an object is moving, it tends to maintain its direction and speed. It will continue to move in a straight line unless acted upon by another, unbalanced force. A person riding in a car travels at the same speed as the car. The person has the same rate of inertia. But if the car stops suddenly, the person's inertia tendency continues at the same speed and direction. The seat belt acts as an outside force to stop the forward movement.

Action and Reaction

Newton's *third law of motion* states that for every action, there is an equal and opposite reaction. When an object pushes or pulls in one direction, the action, there is another push or pull in the opposite direction, the reaction. For example, when a bat hits a baseball, the ball reacts by moving in the opposite direction. If the forces are equal, or balanced, there is no motion. This is exemplified by a book lying on a table. The book is being pulled by the force of gravity, but the table is reacting by pushing up. The result is that the book remains at rest.

Motion

Motion is the movement of an object. We can tell if an object moves by comparing it to something that does not move, a frame of reference. Most motion is compared to the Sun, Moon, stars, or other objects that are far away and appear not to move. You can determine how fast or slow an object moves by measuring its speed. Speed is the distance an object moves in a given amount of time. To calculate speed, use this formula:

$$\text{Speed} = \frac{\text{Distance traveled}}{\text{Time traveled}}$$

Velocity describes the direction of an object. Velocity is the speed of an object in a given direction. It includes both speed and direction. If either speed or direction changes, then velocity changes, too. Motion can also be affected by gravity, outside forces of cables or strings, or a collision between objects. A collision can start or stop a motion or change the direction of a motion.

Acceleration

Any change in the speed or direction of an object is acceleration. Newton's *second law of motion* states that an object accelerates faster as the force gets larger or the object's mass gets smaller. In other words, it takes less force to move an object with a smaller amount of mass. Moreover, if a force pushes or pulls an object in the same direction, there is positive acceleration. Negative acceleration occurs when a force pushes or pulls an object in the opposite direction than it is moving.

Energy

Energy is the ability to cause change. Potential energy is the energy stored in an object because of its position. Objects that bend, stretch, or compress, like a rubber band, have elastic potential energy. Those objects that have the ability to fall, like a roller-coaster car on the brink of a hill, have gravitational potential energy. Potential energy can be converted to kinetic energy, the energy of a moving object. The same roller-coaster car that has gravitational potential energy changes its energy to kinetic energy as soon as it begins to descend.

Electric Energy

Electric energy is a form of energy that creates a force, a push or pull, that causes other objects to move. It is the result of a negative charge when electrons move away from an object or are pushed along a path producing a negative charge. This movement can then be transferred into heat, sound, light, or other kinds of movement.

Static Electricity

Matter is made of tiny particles called atoms. Atoms are composed of protons, electrons, and neutrons. Protons have positive charges, electrons have negative charges, and neutrons have no charge. Protons and neutrons are inside the nucleus of an atom, while electrons orbit around it. If a particle has the same number of positive and negative charges, there is no charge; it is called neutral. Most matter has a neutral charge.

A neutral object can lose electrons when it is rubbed. The charges move in all directions. The negative charges jump to other objects, creating static electricity. Objects that have static electricity attract objects that have opposite charges. They repel those that have the same kind of charge. Sometimes, a plastic comb will create static electricity as the hair is brushed. Negative charges from the comb jump to the hair. Since each hair is similarly charged, it repels the other strands of hair. Sometimes, light objects that have a neutral charge even attract objects with static electricity.

Lightning is another example of static electricity. Extra electrons build up in clouds. As millions of the electrons jump from cloud to cloud, lightning is produced. Lightning strikes materials that conduct electricity, such as metal and water. For these reasons, it is unsafe to be near water or to use the telephone during an electric storm. Lightning also strikes tall objects. If you are caught in a storm, it is unwise to stand under a tree, since lightning would be more likely to strike it. Moreover, the body is a good conductor. A lightning strike in a tree could jump to a person's body.

Current Electricity

Electricity gives us light, sound, heat, and movement. It is caused by matter that has an electric charge—a negative charge. In electricity the matter is negatively charged and moves in the same direction. By moving in one direction, the charge makes a current. The rate that the current flows depends on the number of charges and how much the wire resists the current. Amperes is the scientific unit that measures the amount of electrons moving past a point in a given interval of time.

Most electricity is made by generators. Generators push the charged particles in the same direction through a conductor. A conductor is a material that charged particles can move through easily. Wires are the main conductors of electricity. Water is another material that conducts an electric current. Any material that a current cannot pass through, such as rubber, is an insulator. Rubber generally covers wires to keep the charges moving in one direction. Without the insulator, wires would heat, and the moving energy would be lost.

Electricity is measured in watts. Electric usage is measured in kilowatt-hours. An average of 1,000 kilowatts is used in an hour. Meters on buildings count the number of kilowatt-hours used. They are generally read once each month.

Circuits

A circuit is the path an electric current travels. There are four parts in a circuit: the source, path, switch, and resistor. The charge leaves the energy source, such as a battery or outlet, and moves through a wire to the resistor, which uses the electric charge, such as a light bulb or toaster. It then must follow a separate path back to its source. The switch controls when the electrons flow. If the charge does not return to its original source, the charge builds up, causing the circuit not to work, or to short.

When the circuit is completed, it is called a closed circuit. An open circuit is one in which a part of the path is missing. The charge is unable to follow its complete path. When a switch is off, the circuit is opened; the electric current does not flow. When the switch is on, the circuit is closed, and the current is able to flow.

Series Circuits

A series circuit is made when all parts of the circuit are joined one after the other. The electric current flows in one path. If one part of the circuit is open or broken, the current does not flow to all the other parts. Many resistors may be added to a series circuit. However, the amount of energy flowing through the wires is the same. The resistors must share the available current. The result is that the resistors may not work to full capacity. For example, if there are three light bulbs on a series circuit, all the bulbs will be dimmer than if only one bulb serves as a resistor.

Parallel Circuits

A parallel circuit has more than one path that an electric current can travel. Several resistors are placed on separate paths and are independent of the others. If one resistor is broken or the circuit is open, the others still operate. The current flow increases when there are more paths. If there are too many paths, it is possible for them to overheat and melt, resulting in a fire. Fuses reduce the risk of this hazard in parallel circuits. A fuse is a piece of wire that melts when it gets too hot. When it melts, the circuit opens, and the flow of electricity stops. Circuit breakers also serve as a safety device. They open the circuit to break the flow of electricity.

Magnetism

Magnetism is a force that attracts metal materials like iron, steel, nickel, and cobalt. This force is found naturally in lodestone rock or magnatite. Magnets attract, or pull, and repel, or push, other pieces of metal. Synthetic magnets are made from steel or a combination of aluminum, nickel, cobalt, and iron. It is easy to transfer a magnetic charge to iron, but the charge will not last. Proper storage of synthetic magnets is important for them to retain their force.

Magnets come in all shapes and sizes. The force is focused at the ends, or poles, of the magnets. These poles have a north and a south side. Most magnets are marked with an N and an S to identify the poles. (However, if they are not marked on a bar magnet, hang the magnet from a string. The north end of the magnet will point toward the north.) Like ends of two magnets repel each other. In other words, if two north ends of magnets are held together, they will repel each other. Unlike ends, a south and a north end, attract each other. The area between the poles has some magnetic force, too, but it is not as strong as the poles.

Magnets do not need to touch, though. There is a magnetic force around each magnet called a magnetic field. When a piece of metal comes within a certain distance of the magnet, the magnet's field starts to pull the metal. The pull increases as the metal gets closer to the magnet. The size of the magnet affects the strength of the magnetic field.

Magnets can also produce an electric charge. When moved back and forth inside a metal coil, magnets produce electricity. Generators were developed based on this principle. They create electricity by moving either a coil of wire through a magnetic field or by moving a magnet through wire coils.

Electromagnets

As electric charges move through a wire, a magnetic field is created around the wire. It is this force that is used to make an electromagnet. A metal bar is wrapped in wire and connected to an electric source, such as a dry cell. The more wire used, the greater the magnetic field and the stronger the magnet will be. Electromagnets have switches so the magnetic field can be turned on and off. Doorbells and cranes in junkyards use the energy of electromagnets.

RELATED READING

- *Acids and Bases* by Chris Oxlade (Chemicals in Action Series, Heinemann, 2002).

- *Circuits, Shocks, and Lightning: The Science of Electricity* by Celeste Peters (Science at Work Series, Raintree Steck-Vaughn, 2000).

- *The Drop in My Drink: The Story of Water on Our Planet* by Meredith Hooper (Viking, 1998).

- *Electric Mischief: Battery-Powered Gadgets Kids Can Build* by Alan Bartholomew (Kids Can Press Ltd., 2002).

- *Electricity and Magnetism* by Steve Parker (Science Fact Files Series, Raintree Steck-Vaughn, 2001).

- *Forces and Motion* by Peter Lafferty (Science Fact Files Series, Raintree Steck-Vaughn, 2001).

- *The New Way Things Work* by David Macauley (Houghton Mifflin, 1998).

- *Separating Materials* by Robert Sneddan (Material World Series, Heinemann, 2001).

- *The Story of Oxygen* by Karen Fitzgerald (First Books Series, Franklin Watts, 1996).

- *Waves: The Electromagnetic Universe* by Gloria Skurzynski (National Geographic, 1996).

Unit 1 Assessment

Read each statement. Write *T* on the line if the statement is true. Write *F* if the statement is false.

_____ 1. Gas molecules only move by vibrating.

_____ 2. The weight in a substance decreases after a chemical reaction.

_____ 3. A balance is used to measure mass.

_____ 4. Motion is described by comparing a moving object to a reference point.

_____ 5. Objects in motion tend to keep moving unless some force acts on them to stop them.

_____ 6. A car can accelerate by changing its speed.

_____ 7. Lightning is an example of static electricity.

_____ 8. Copper is a good insulator.

Darken the letter of the answer that best completes each sentence.

9. Since lemon juice is an acid, it will change _____.
   Ⓐ blue litmus paper to pink
   Ⓑ pink litmus paper to blue
   Ⓒ blue litmus paper to purple
   Ⓓ pink litmus paper to purple

10. Hydrogen and oxygen make _____.
    Ⓐ carbon dioxide
    Ⓑ salt
    Ⓒ mercuric oxide
    Ⓓ water

11. An example of a chemical reaction is _____.
    Ⓐ a burning fire
    Ⓑ a reaction between baking soda and vinegar
    Ⓒ rusting iron
    Ⓓ all of the above

12. The smallest part of a substance that has all the properties of that substance is _____.
    Ⓐ a base
    Ⓑ a molecule
    Ⓒ an atom
    Ⓓ an acid

GO ON TO THE NEXT PAGE ☞

Unit 1 Assessment, p. 2

Darken the letter of the answer that best completes each sentence.

13. Lemonade is an example of a _____.
  Ⓐ colloid
  Ⓑ compound
  Ⓒ solution
  Ⓓ molecule

14. When two substances go through a chemical change, _____.
  Ⓐ they always turn into gases
  Ⓑ their physical properties remain the same
  Ⓒ their molecules remain the same
  Ⓓ they form a new substance with different properties

15. The speed of a car that travels 150 kilometers in 3 hours is _____.
  Ⓐ 50 kph
  Ⓑ 450 kph
  Ⓒ 75 kph
  Ⓓ 55 kph

16. The amount of inertia an object has depends on its _____.
  Ⓐ mass
  Ⓑ speed
  Ⓒ motion
  Ⓓ size

17. The force of gravity opposes the force of _____.
  Ⓐ friction
  Ⓑ inertia
  Ⓒ energy
  Ⓓ acceleration

18. The action and reaction forces are equal when a basketball is _____.
  Ⓐ resting on the floor
  Ⓑ falling through the hoop
  Ⓒ being dribbled
  Ⓓ passed from one player to another

19. Static electricity is produced when _____.
  Ⓐ objects lose all their charges
  Ⓑ negative charges become positive charges
  Ⓒ negative charges move from one object to another
  Ⓓ positive charges move from one object to another

20. The difference between electromagnets and regular magnets is that electromagnets _____.
  Ⓐ have a magnetic force
  Ⓑ can be turned on and off
  Ⓒ attract different materials
  Ⓓ have north and south poles

Matter

Matter is made up of basic units. Matter can be combined, separated, mixed, and altered. The smallest building block of matter that retains the properties of matter is the **atom**. A single crystal of salt or grain of rice is made up of millions of atoms. Atoms are too small to be seen except with very powerful microscopes.

An **element** is made up of only one kind of atom. Few of the things you see around you are pure elements. Wood, plastic, and steel are made of molecules that consist of many kinds of atoms. A substance made of two or more elements chemically combined is called a **compound**. When two or more atoms combine, they form a **molecule**. A molecule is the smallest particle of matter that consists of more than one atom.

Darken the letter of the answer that best completes each sentence.

1. The smallest building block of matter is _____.
  Ⓐ a molecule
  Ⓑ an element
  Ⓒ an atom
  Ⓓ a compound

2. _____ is made up of only one kind of atom.
  Ⓐ A molecule
  Ⓑ An element
  Ⓒ An atom
  Ⓓ A compound

3. _____ is a substance made of two or more elements chemically combined.
  Ⓐ A molecule
  Ⓑ An element
  Ⓒ An atom
  Ⓓ A compound

4. When two or more atoms combine, they form _____.
  Ⓐ a molecule
  Ⓑ an element
  Ⓒ an atom
  Ⓓ a compound

Properties of Matter

Everything we see, touch, taste, and smell is matter. Matter is anything that has mass and takes up space. We can tell different substances, or objects of matter, apart by their characteristics, or **properties**. Some of these properties are color, taste, and odor. Some properties of a substance always stay the same. For example, the color, taste, and smell of an orange are the same whether the orange is small or large, whole or sliced.

Another way that matter can be described is by measurement. You use measurements in almost everything you do. When everyone agrees to use the same units of measurement, they are using standard units. Scientists from around the world have adopted the International System of Units, or SI, for a standard of measurement. This standard is sometimes called the metric system. People use these standard units to make all kinds of measurements every day. For example, cooking requires measuring volume, or the amount of space something takes up. When you measure the amount of matter in an object, you are measuring **mass**. People often confuse mass with **weight**, which is a measure of the force of gravity pulling on an object. Weight varies with the gravitational force on an object, but mass remains the same.

Answer these questions.

1. Describe what matter is. _____

_____

_____

2. Describe an orange according to its properties. _____

_____

_____

_____

3. Why do we measure using standard units instead of measuring with any kind of units?

_____

_____

_____

_____

Phases of Matter

Matter can also be found in solid, liquid, and gas states, or **phases**. Some matter can go through all three phase changes as a result of heating or cooling. Water, for example, forms a solid at freezing temperatures, and when heated, melts into a liquid. As a liquid, water can change into a gas through evaporation and can once again, through cooling, become a liquid by condensation.

 Answer the questions.

1. In the boxes below, show which is the solid, liquid, or gas by labeling each.

 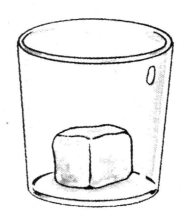 

a. _____ b. _____ c. _____

2. Explain why condensation forms on a glass containing a cold drink.

_____

_____

_____

_____

3. Explain how evaporation occurs.

_____

_____

_____

_____

Molecules in Matter

The three phases of matter are solids, liquids, and gases. Molecules are the smallest parts of a substance. In solids, molecules are packed tightly together, vibrating slightly. For this reason, solids retain their shape. In liquids, molecules are packed less tightly; they slide over each other. Therefore, water has the characteristics of size and movement. In gases, molecules bump against each other, moving wildly and quickly in all directions. Gas does not have its own shape and must take the shape of its container.

 Look at the pictures. Tell which is a picture of the molecules in a solid, liquid, or gas. Write *solid, liquid,* or *gas*.

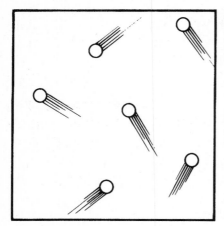 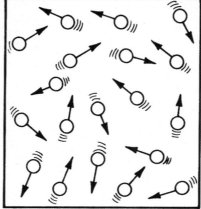 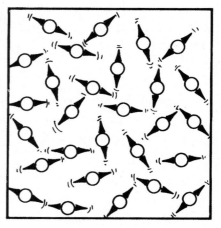

1. _____   2. _____   3. _____

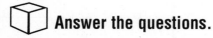 **Answer the questions.**

4. In which kind of matter do the molecules move the fastest?

_____

5. In which kind of matter do the molecules vibrate?

_____

6. Compare the movement of molecules in a solid with the movement of molecules in a liquid.

_____

_____

Heat

Heat is the transfer of thermal energy. It can be measured as the total kinetic energy of the motion of the atoms or molecules in a substance.

We know that all matter is made of tiny particles called molecules. These particles are in constant motion. Scientists know that heat is a form of energy. As an object becomes hotter, its atoms and molecules move faster. You can determine how hot something is by taking its temperature. **Temperature** is the measure of the average kinetic energy, or energy of movement, of the atoms and molecules in a substance or an object.

Conduction is the movement of heat that occurs when atoms or molecules bump into one another. Through contact, kinetic energy, in the form of heat, is transferred. **Convection** is the transfer of heat by currents of molecules in liquids and gases. As water nears a heat source, it becomes hotter; its molecules begin moving faster and spreading out. The warmer water is less dense than the cooler water, so the warmer water is pushed up by the cooler, more dense water. This produces currents of warm water that carry heat.

In conduction and convection, the movement of molecules transfers heat. The Sun's heat does not require the movement of molecules. Instead, the heat is transferred by **radiation**, or by infrared rays. Infrared rays are like light rays, but they cannot be seen. These rays travel in straight lines as fast as light. The Sun's rays travel through space to Earth and produce radiant heat.

Answer these questions.

1. How is heat related to temperature?

   _____

   _____

   _____

2. What happens to solids, liquids, and gases when they are heated?

   _____

   _____

   _____

GO ON TO THE NEXT PAGE ☞

Heat, p. 2

 Answer these questions.

3. Label the appropriate molecule models as *solid, liquid,* or *gas.*

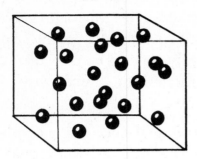 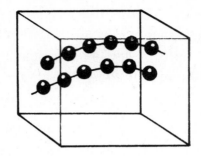 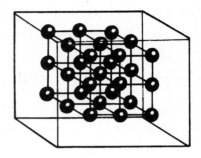

_____ _____ _____

4. Explain how heat movement by conduction occurs.

_____

_____

5. Explain how heat movement by convection occurs.

_____

_____

6. Explain why heat energy from the Sun reaches the Earth only by radiation.

_____

_____

_____

Darken the letter of the answer that best completes each sentence.

7. _____ is a form of energy that is produced by the movement of molecules in a substance.
- Ⓐ Temperature
- Ⓑ Conduction
- Ⓒ Heat
- Ⓓ Radiation

8. _____ is the measure of the average kinetic energy of the molecules in a substance or an object.
- Ⓐ Temperature
- Ⓑ Conduction
- Ⓒ Heat
- Ⓓ Radiation

Name _____ Date _____

Measuring Mass

A **balance** is used to measure a solid object's mass. Balances have two pans. In one pan you place the object you want to measure. In the other you place the gram (g) weights, the metric units used by scientists to measure mass. Do this activity to learn more about using a balance.

You will need

☆ balance scale   ☆ gram weights   ☆ 4 or 5 objects

1. Make sure the empty pans are balanced. They are in balance if the pointer is at the middle mark on the base. If the pointer is not at this mark, move the slider to the right or left.

2. Place one object in a pan. The pointer will move toward the pan that is empty.

3. Place weights carefully in the empty pan. The pointer will move back toward the middle. When the pointer returns to the middle, the pans are balanced. Add the numbers on the gram weights. The total is the mass of the object.

4. Repeat with the other objects. Fill in the chart as you go.

MEASURING MASS

Object	Mass (g)

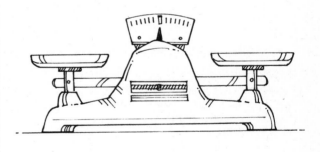

Answer the questions.

1. Why must the pointer be in the middle before you begin?

_____

2. How do you find the mass of an object once the scale is balanced?

_____

3. List your items in order from the least mass to the most mass.

_____

Measuring the Volume of a Solid

Volume is how much space an object takes up. For objects that have a regular shape with straight sides, like a box, you use a ruler and this formula: *length x width x height = volume*. The scientific unit to measure volume is cubic centimeters (cm^3). For objects that have an irregular shape, like a rock, you will need to use a measuring cup of water and the scientific unit of milliliters (mL). One cubic centimeter equals one milliliter. Do this activity to learn more about measuring volume.

You will need

☆ metric ruler ☆ measuring cup ☆ water ☆ string ☆ 4 or 5 objects

1. For the objects with straight sides, use the ruler to measure their length, width, and height. Find their volume by multiplying these numbers together. Record the volume in the chart. (Remember to use the correct scientific unit.)

2. For objects with irregular sides, fill a measuring cup half full with water. Note the water level. Tie a string around the object and lower it into the cup. Be sure the object is totally under water. Subtract the first water level from the second. The difference is the object's volume. Record the volume in the chart.

MEASURING VOLUME

Object	Volume (cm³ or mL)

Answer the questions.

1. Which method would you use to find the volume of a fish tank? Explain.

_____

_____

2. Which method would you use to find the volume of a set of keys? Explain.

_____

_____

3. List your items in order from the least volume to the most volume.

_____

_____

Measuring Density

Density tells you how much mass is in a certain volume. To find the density, you need to know the mass and volume of the object. You then divide the mass of the object by its volume.

$$\text{Density} = \frac{\text{Mass}}{\text{Volume}}$$

The units of density are grams per milliliter or grams per cubic centimeter. These units are written as g/mL and g/cc. You can compare densities of different materials. Do this activity to learn more about measuring density.

You will need

- ☆ balance scale   ☆ gram weights   ☆ metric measuring cup
- ☆ materials to measure, such as milk, corn oil, syrup   ☆ water

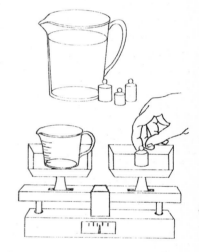

1. Using the balance scale, find the mass of the measuring cup.

   What is its mass? _____

2. Fill the measuring cup with exactly 100 mL of water. Find the mass of the water and the cup together.

   What is it? _____

3. To find the mass of the water, subtract the mass of the measuring cup from the total mass of the cup and the water.

   What is the mass of the water? _____

4. Now you can find the density of water. Divide the mass of the water by the volume of water.

   What is the density? _____

5. Find the density of other liquids, such as milk and corn oil. Fill in the chart below.

MEASURING DENSITY

Name of Liquid	Mass of Measuring Cup	Mass of Liquid and Measuring Cup	Mass of Liquid	Volume	Density
water					

Name _____ Date _____

Changes in Matter

There are two ways matter can change—chemically and physically. When elements combine to form a compound, a **chemical change** occurs. In a chemical change, a new chemical is formed from another type of matter. Burning charcoal is an example of a chemical change.

A **physical change** in matter is a change that does not form a new chemical. Examples of physical changes are boiling, dissolving, evaporating, and freezing.

Answer the questions.

1. Explain the difference between a chemical change and a physical change.

_____

_____

_____

_____

2. List some clues that a chemical change has occurred.

_____

_____

_____

_____

3. Identify each example as a chemical change or a physical change.

Example	Type of Change
Cutting strawberries	
Baking a cake	

Mixtures

In a **mixture**, the parts keep their properties, even though the parts are mixed together. A **solution** is a mixture in which the composition is the same throughout. A **suspension** is a solution in which one of the parts is a liquid. Suspensions are very common in everyday life.

When you are making a gelatin dessert mold, you are making another type of mixture. The gelatin in the dessert is a mixture called a colloid. In a **colloid**, the parts do not dissolve, but they are so small that they do not settle out. They remain suspended because they are constantly moving.

Answer the questions.

1. In _____ the parts keep their own properties.
   - Ⓐ a suspension
   - Ⓑ a solution
   - Ⓒ a mixture
   - Ⓓ a colloid

2. _____ are mixtures in which the composition is the same throughout.
   - Ⓐ Suspensions
   - Ⓑ Solutions
   - Ⓒ Mixtures
   - Ⓓ Colloids

3. _____ is a mixture in which one of the parts is a liquid.
   - Ⓐ A suspension
   - Ⓑ A solution
   - Ⓒ A mixture
   - Ⓓ A colloid

4. _____ is a mixture in which the particles do not settle out.
   - Ⓐ A suspension
   - Ⓑ A solution
   - Ⓒ A mixture
   - Ⓓ A colloid

5. Describe what the *solvent* and *solute* of a solution are. Use a reference book to help you.

_____

_____

_____

_____

_____

_____

_____

Compounds

A **compound** results when two or more elements combine chemically. As a result, you end up with something you didn't have before. Rust is a compound. Rust results from the combining of atoms of the element oxygen in air with atoms of the element iron.

Water is also a compound. Each molecule of the compound water is made up of two atoms of hydrogen and one atom of oxygen. Hydrogen and oxygen are gases, but when they combine as H_2O, they form the clear liquid water.

Another example of a compound is salt. Salt is made up of the elements sodium and chlorine. As an element, sodium is a solid that is dangerous to handle because it can burst into flames. Chlorine is a poisonous gas. But when sodium and chlorine are combined chemically in the ratio of one to one, they form salt (NaCl), a white crystal that is safe to handle and eat.

Answer the questions.

1. Explain the difference between a mixture and a compound.

_____

_____

_____

_____

2. Explain how the compound water is formed.

_____

_____

_____

_____

Name _____ Date _____

Word Equations

Chemists have a special way of writing about chemical changes. They write **word equations** instead of complete sentences. In a word equation, a few words and math symbols tell what happens. For example, here is a word equation that tells what happens when an iron nail rusts.

iron + oxygen ⟶ iron oxide

It is read this way: "Iron and oxygen become iron oxide." The name *iron oxide* tells you two things. It tells you that iron is part of the compound. The word *oxide* tells you that oxygen also is part of the compound. The arrow means "becomes."

Word equations also can be used to show that a compound may be broken down into its elements. For example, here is a word equation that tells about salt. Another name for salt is sodium chloride.

sodium chloride ⟶ sodium + chlorine

It is read this way: "Sodium chloride becomes sodium and chlorine."

 What do these word equations say?

1. carbon + oxygen ⟶ carbon dioxide

_____

2. hydrogen + oxygen ⟶ water

_____

3. mercuric oxide ⟶ mercury + oxygen

_____

4. iron sulfide ⟶ iron + sulfur

_____

 Complete these word equations.

5. calcium chloride ⟶ _____ + chlorine

6. _____ + oxygen ⟶ zinc oxide

Making Carbon Dioxide

Carbon dioxide is a compound made from carbon and oxygen. When carbon and oxygen are combined, a chemical change occurs. The compound carbon dioxide is formed. You can make carbon dioxide by combining baking soda and vinegar. These two substances contain the elements carbon and oxygen. When baking soda and vinegar are mixed, the carbon and oxygen join to form carbon dioxide. Make carbon dioxide and learn about its density in this activity.

You will need

- ⭐ large jar
- ⭐ unpopped popcorn kernels
- ⭐ spoon
- ⭐ water
- ⭐ baking soda
- ⭐ measuring spoons
- ⭐ vinegar
- ⭐ measuring cup

1. Pour 350 mL of water into the jar. Add 2 teaspoons of baking soda. Stir until the baking soda dissolves.

2. Add about 30 kernels of popcorn. What happens?

   _____

   What does this tell you about the density of popcorn?

   _____

3. Pour 45 mL of vinegar into the water. Stir gently. What happens?

   _____

   These bubbles are carbon dioxide gas. What do the bubbles do?

   _____

   What does this tell you about the density of carbon dioxide?

   _____

4. Watch the popcorn for a few minutes. What happens?

   _____

   What does this tell you about the density of the popcorn-bubble combination?

   _____

How Can You Separate Compounds?

Compounds can be separated. For example, you can separate the color dye compound in felt-tip markers.

You will need

⭐ various colored felt-tip markers   ⭐ a paper towel   ⭐ water

⭐ a pair of scissors   ⭐ a baby food jar

1. Cut out circles from white paper towels. The circles should be 10 cm in diameter. Cut a narrow tail into the center of each circle as shown in Figure 1. Put a spot of color from a marker at the top of the tail. Use a different color on each circle.

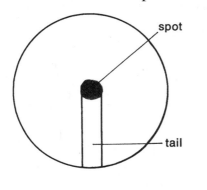

Figure 1

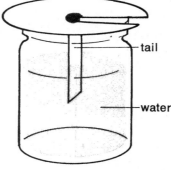

Figure 2

2. Bend the tail of one circle downward. Set it in a baby food jar full of water as shown in Figure 2. Watch the dye spread.

3. Write the color of the marker and the color or colors of the dye compounds in the table below.

4. Remove the circle from the top of the jar. Replace it with a circle that has a different-colored spot. Repeat steps 2–4 until you have tested all the circles.

DYE COMPOUNDS

Color of Marker	Dye Compounds in Marker

Acids and Bases

Compounds can be divided into two groups: **acids** and **bases**. There are many kinds of acids and bases in your home and school. **Litmus paper** can be used to test a substance chemically to discover which compound it is. Litmus paper comes in colors of blue and pink. A substance that is a base will change pink litmus to blue. A substance that is an acid will change blue litmus to pink. If both strips stay the same color, then the substance is neutral. It is neither a base nor an acid. You will test acids and bases in this activity.

You will need

- ★ pink and blue litmus paper
- ★ 5 small paper cups
- ★ lemon juice
- ★ milk
- ★ carbonated drink
- ★ sugar water
- ★ dish soap
- ★ marker

1. Label each cup with the name of a different substance. Pour a small amount of milk into its cup. Repeat with the other four liquids.

2. Dip a strip of blue litmus into the milk. Did it change color? Record your findings in the chart.

3. Dip a strip of pink litmus into the same cup. Did it change color? Record your findings in the chart.

4. Record whether milk is a base, an acid, or a neutral in the last column of the chart.

5. Repeat steps 2–4 with the other four liquids.

TESTING HOUSEHOLD SUBSTANCES

Material	Reaction to blue litmus paper	Reaction to pink litmus paper	What substance is
Milk			
Lemon juice			
Dish soap			
Sugar water			
Carbonated drink			

Does the Amount of Matter Change After a Chemical Reaction?

When matter changes form in a chemical reaction, it will look, smell, and feel different. However, nothing is lost or gained. The substance should have the same mass. Do the activity to see if this is true.

You will need

- ★ baking soda
- ★ empty pill bottle
- ★ small funnel
- ★ vinegar
- ★ teaspoon
- ★ balance scale
- ★ balloon
- ★ gram weights

---

1. Pour one teaspoon of baking soda through the funnel into the balloon.

2. Fill the pill bottle half full with vinegar.

3. Pull the opening of the balloon over the mouth of the bottle.

4. Put the balloon and bottle on one side of the balance scale. Add weights to the other side until the balance is level.

5. Remove the balloon and bottle from the scale. Pour the baking soda from the balloon into the pill bottle of vinegar. Observe what happens.

6. Repeat Step 4.

 Answer the questions.

1. What happened when you mixed the baking soda and the vinegar in Step 5?

   _____

2. Did the balance remain level after replacing the balloon and bottle on the balance in Step 6?

   _____

3. Was the amount of matter the same both before and after the chemical reaction? Explain.

   _____

   _____

The Direction of Force

What do you think of when you hear the word *work*? Do you think about playing on the playground? Probably not. Yet, when you use playground or exercise equipment, you are doing work. You do work when you use force to move an object.

A **force** is a push or a pull. Forces have magnitude and direction. A force can start an object moving, change the direction and rate of its motion, or change the shape of the object. Any force acts in a specific direction with a specific size or strength. Forces can be combined to increase their effect. You can illustrate a force by using an arrow. The head of the arrow shows the direction of the force. The tail of the arrow identifies the point where the force is coming from.

Look at the picture. Draw arrows to indicate the direction of the forces and where they are coming from.

1.

Identify the following activities as pushes or pulls. Write *push* or *pull* on the line.

_____ **2.**	hitting a tennis ball	
_____ **3.**	painting a wall	
_____ **4.**	brushing your teeth	
_____ **5.**	brushing your hair	

_____ **6.** writing with a pencil

_____ **7.** rowing a boat

_____ **8.** pedaling a bicycle

_____ **9.** climbing a rope

Can You Observe the Direction of Opposite Forces?

Forces always occur together. When there is one force, whether an object is still or moving, there is another force working in the opposite direction—a reaction. Newton's *third law of motion* states that for every **action**, there is an equal and opposite **reaction**. Find out more in this activity.

You will need

☆ scissors   ☆ 1-qt (1-liter) milk carton   ☆ balloon   ☆ tape

☆ sink or tub filled with water 5 cm deep

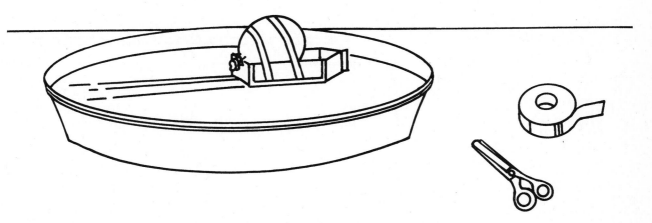

1. Cut the milk carton in half lengthwise. Cut a small notch in the bottom of the milk carton.

2. Blow up the balloon, but do not tie it.

3. While holding the air of the balloon in, tape the balloon in the milk carton. Place the end you are holding into the notch.

4. Put the carton in a tub of water.

5. Release the balloon so the air flows out of the balloon.

Answer these questions on another piece of paper.

1. Which way did the air coming out of the balloon move?
2. Which way did the carton move?
3. Which force was the action force?
4. Which force was the reaction force?
5. What scientific law did you observe in this activity?
6. How is the force of the air in the balloon like a propeller in a boat?

The Force of Gravity

Gravity is the force that pulls objects in the universe toward one another. Earth is surrounded by a gravitational field that decreases in strength as the distance from Earth increases. The size of the force of gravity between any two objects is determined by the masses of the objects and the distance between them. Mass is the amount of matter. Learn more about gravity in this activity.

You will need

☆ Ping-Pong ball   ☆ golf ball   ☆ large marble

☆ rubber ball (from jacks)   ☆ ruler   ☆ small wooden ball

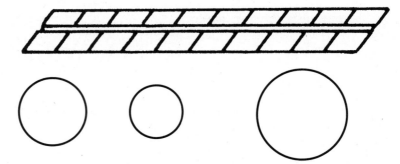

1. Work with a partner. Choose three balls.

2. Place all three balls on the edge of the table about 4 cm apart. Predict which ball will hit the ground first when all are pushed off the table at the same time.

3. Hold the ruler so that the side with numbers faces the balls. Gently push the balls off the table at the same time. Your partner should look at the floor to see which ball hits the floor first.

4. Record your observation in the chart.

5. Repeat Steps 2 and 3 two more times. Record your observations in the chart.

BALL DROP

Trial	Observation
Trial 1	
Trial 2	
Trial 3	

Answer these questions on another piece of paper.

1. What did you observe about the order in which the balls hit the ground?

2. How is the force of gravity acting on the balls related to their mass?

3. How is gravity a force?

Name _____   Date _____

How Much Force?

A **newton** is the unit used to measure force. One newton (N) is equal to the force of Earth's gravity on a 100-gram (g) mass. This means that if you are on Earth and you want to lift a 100-gram mass, you would have to exert a force of 1 newton.

The chart below shows how much force would be required to lift various objects on Earth as well as on two other planets, called Planet X and Planet Y.

FORCE TO LIFT OBJECTS

Object	Force Required to Lift on Earth (N)	Force Required to Lift on Planet X (N)	Force Required to Lift on Planet Y (N)	Mass (g)
1	20	8	4	2,000
2	7.5	3	1.5	750
3	12.5	5	2.5	1,250
4	5	2	1	500
5	25	10	5	2,500

Study the table, and then answer the questions on another piece of paper.

1. Which of the three planets has the strongest gravitational pull? Explain.
2. Which of the three planets has the weakest gravitational pull? Explain.
3. Write a mathematical sentence that describes the relationship between the gravitational force on Earth and the gravitational force on planet Y.
4. Write a mathematical sentence that describes the relationship between the gravitational force on Earth and the gravitational force on planet X.
5. Write a mathematical sentence that describes the relationship between the gravitational force on planet X and on planet Y.
6. Which object listed has the greatest mass on Earth? Explain.
7. List the objects in order, from the one having the greatest mass to the one having the least mass.
8. Which object has four times the mass of which other object?

How Does Force Change Motion?

Forces can affect the motion of objects. Gravity is a force that acts on all objects in the universe. Gravity can affect the motion of a baseball that is thrown. Gravity causes an object to change direction as it falls.

Circular motion, such as a swinging ride at an amusement park, can be affected by the force of cables holding the cars. The collision of objects can affect motion, also. A collision can start motion, stop motion, change the speed of motion, or change the direction of motion.

Look at the diagrams below. Describe the force that is affecting the motion in each case.

1.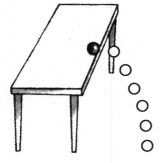

_____

_____

_____

_____

2.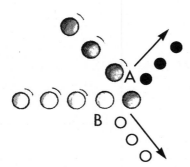

_____

_____

_____

_____

3.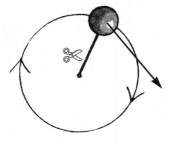

_____

_____

_____

_____

Balanced and Unbalanced Forces

Some forces result in movement, and some do not. Two forces that are equal in size but opposite in direction are **balanced forces**. Balanced forces do not change the position of an object. To cause a change in motion, forces must be unbalanced. **Unbalanced forces** are opposite and unequal. Find out about these kinds of forces in this activity.

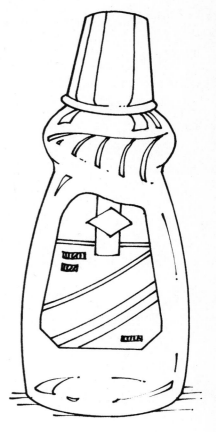

You will need
★ water

★ tissue paper

★ small paper cup

★ empty squeezable detergent bottle

1. Moisten a small piece of tissue paper and shape it into a plug for the hole in the top of the bottle. Place it in the hole to plug the bottle.

2. Place the cup upside down over the bottle.

3. Squeeze the bottle as hard as you can. Observe what happens.

Answer the questions.

1. What two forces were acting to cause what you observed?

_____

_____

2. How did the two forces compare in their direction and size?

_____

_____

3. Could balanced forces have caused what you observed? Explain.

_____

_____

_____

Kinds of Energy

Motion involves energy. **Energy** is the ability to cause change. At the top of a hill, a roller coaster has **potential energy**—the energy stored in an object. As the roller coaster descends, its potential energy is converted to **kinetic energy**, the energy of movement. The energy stored in an object that can bend or stretch and then return to its original shape is called elastic potential energy. This energy can be observed in items such as a rubber band or a stretched spring. The energy an object has because of its ability to fall is gravitational potential energy. A marble held above the floor has this kind of potential energy. When you drop the marble, the gravitational potential energy is converted into kinetic energy. The higher you hold the marble, the greater the energy it has.

An object in motion has **momentum**. An object's momentum is its mass multiplied by its velocity. If its mass or velocity is large, an object will have a large momentum. The more momentum an object has, the harder it is to stop the object or to change its direction.

Darken the letter of the best answer.

1. A diver poised on a diving board has _____.
   Ⓐ kinetic energy
   Ⓑ mechanical energy
   Ⓒ gravitational potential energy
   Ⓓ elastic potential energy

2. As the diver jumps, the board bends down. At this point the board has _____.
   Ⓐ kinetic energy
   Ⓑ mechanical energy
   Ⓒ gravitational potential energy
   Ⓓ elastic potential energy

3. As the diver plunges into the water, the diver has _____.
   Ⓐ kinetic energy
   Ⓑ mechanical energy
   Ⓒ gravitational potential energy
   Ⓓ elastic potential energy

4. Which has the greatest momentum?
   Ⓐ a bowling ball traveling at 10 kilometers per hour (kph)
   Ⓑ a bowling ball traveling at 20 kph
   Ⓒ a basketball traveling at 10 kph
   Ⓓ a basketball traveling at 20 kph

Where Is the Frame of Reference?

The physical world is constantly in motion. Each time you describe something that is moving, you are comparing it with another object or a background that you assume is not moving. This background or object is your **frame of reference**. The most basic frame of reference we use is the movement of the Earth around the Sun. Even ancient people observed the Earth's relationship to the Sun and the stars. They built structures, such as Casa Grande in Arizona, to observe the apparent movement of the Sun and the stars. Find out more about the frame of reference in this activity.

You will need

☆ pencil

1. Hold the pencil out front at arm's length. Close one eye.

2. Move your head and the pencil to the left and then to the right. What appears to move?

3. Now, move your head left and right, but hold the pencil still. What appears to move?

Answer the questions.

1. In Step 2, what appears to be moving?

_____

2. What is the frame of reference?

_____

3. In Step 3, what appears to be moving?

_____

4. What is the frame of reference?

_____

How Do You Measure the Speed of a Marble?

Speed is the distance an object moves in a certain amount of time. To find speed, use this formula:

$$\text{Speed} = \frac{\text{distance traveled}}{\text{time traveled}}$$

You will need

★ glass marble   ★ ruler with pencil groove   ★ meter stick   ★ book

★ masking tape   ★ a stopwatch or clock with second hand

1. Work with a partner. Put the book on the floor. Place the end of the ruler on the edge of the book to make a ramp.

2. Measure 5 m from one edge of the book across the floor. Mark the point with a piece of tape.

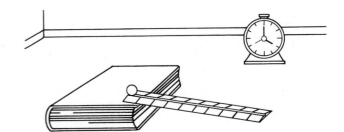

3. Have your partner look at the second hand of the clock. When your partner says "Go," let the marble go from the top of the ramp.

4. As the marble rolls toward the tape, your partner should count the seconds that go by. When the marble reaches the tape, you should say "Stop."

5. Record the distance and the time in the chart. Use the formula to find the speed of the marble. Record the speed in the chart.

6. Repeat Steps 3–5 for three more trials.

MARBLE SPEED

Trial	Distance	Time (sec)	Speed (m/sec)
1			
2			
3			
4			

Answer these questions on another piece of paper.

1. Was the speed the same for each trial?
2. If the speeds were different, find the average speed by adding the speeds and dividing by 4.
3. Explain why an average speed should be found.
4. What factor caused the speed of the rolling marble to change from one trial to the next?

Velocity

You are probably familiar with the formula *Speed = distance ÷ time*. You use this formula to find how fast an object such as a car is moving. If the length of the sidewalk in front of your school is 61 meters (200 feet), and you can ride your bike the length of the walk in 18 seconds, then your speed is 61 meters divided by 18 seconds, or 3.4 meters per second (11 feet per second).

Velocity is a term that refers to both speed and direction. If you are going east when you ride in front of the school, then your velocity is 3.4 meters per second east. You could also express the velocity as 12.2 kilometers per hour east, abbreviated as 12.2 km/hr east (7.6 miles per hour east, 7.6 mi/hr east).

An object traveling parallel to another has, in addition to its own velocity, a velocity relative to the object traveling with it. For example, suppose that one car passes another on a highway. The first car has a velocity of 80 km/hr (50 mi/hr) east. The second car has a velocity of 97 km/hr (60 mi/hr) east. How fast is the second car going relative to the first car? To find out, subtract the first velocity from the second: 97 − 80 = 17 km/hr east. In other words, the second car is pulling ahead of the first one at the rate of 17 km/hr east. Knowing this, you can calculate how much earlier the second car will arrive at a certain point.

Objects traveling in opposite directions also have velocities relative to each other. Suppose a train left New York and was traveling at a rate of 129 km/hr (80 mi/hr) west. At the same time, a train left Chicago and was traveling east at a rate of 112 km/hr (70 mi/hr) east. To find how fast they were traveling relative to each other, or how fast the gap between them was closing, add the two velocities. The gap between these two trains was closing at a rate of 129 + 112 = 241 km/hr (150 mi/hr).

GO ON TO THE NEXT PAGE ☞

Velocity, p. 2

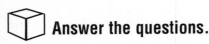 **Answer the questions.**

1. John and Tom live near each other and work at the same job. John leaves for work at 7 A.M. and drives at a velocity of 48 km/hr (30 mi/hr) east. Tom leaves 15 minutes later and drives at a velocity of 64 km/hr (40 mi/hr) east.

   What is Tom's velocity relative to John's? _____

2. Why do we subtract when calculating relative velocities of vehicles traveling in the same direction? _____

   _____

   _____

   _____

3. In what way could it be useful to know the relative velocities of vehicles traveling in parallel? _____

   _____

   _____

   _____

4. Mary and Yolanda live at opposite ends of town, and they recently decided to meet for lunch. They left their homes at the same time. Mary was traveling at a velocity of 56 km/hr (35 mi/hr) east. Yolanda had to go through town, where there is a speed limit of 40 km/hr (25 mi/hr).

   How fast was the gap closing between them? _____

5. An airplane leaves New York bound for California. Its airspeed is 1,030 km/hr (640 mi/hr). At the same time, an airplane leaves California bound for New York. They are heading toward each other (at different altitudes) at a speed of 2,042 km/hr (1,269 mi/hr).

   What is the velocity of the eastbound airplane? _____

Inertia

All things have **inertia**. Read these three facts about inertia:

A. An object at rest tends to stay at rest.

B. Once in motion, an object remains in motion in a straight line.

C. A moving object continues to move in a straight line unless acted upon by an outside force.

 Look at the pictures below, and read about each one. Decide which of the above facts best describes each picture. Write _A._, _B._, or _C._ on the line below each picture.

1.

_____

When a moving car stops suddenly, the people in it keep moving.

4.

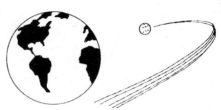

_____

Gravitation pulls on the Moon. This causes it to revolve around Earth in a circular path.

2.

_____

The ball is not moving.

5.

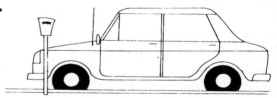

_____

The car remains in one place.

3.

_____

The child moves down the slide.

6.

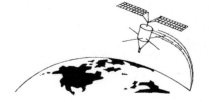

_____

The satellite orbits Earth.

How Can You Compare the Inertia of Two Objects?

The amount of matter in an object is its mass. More mass in an object also means that it has more inertia. More force will be needed to move it because it has a greater tendency to remain at rest. Learn more about inertia in this activity.

You will need

- ★ steel washer, 4–5 cm in diameter
- ★ 30-cm metal strip
- ★ rubber band
- ★ 3 books
- ★ clock with second hand
- ★ rock, 2–4 cm in diameter

1. Work with a partner. Use the rubber band to attach the washer to the metal strip.

2. Stack the three books on the edge of a table.

3. Place 10 cm of the strip underneath the books.

4. Push the washer end of the strip down about 5 cm. Have your partner look at the second hand of the clock. When your partner says "Go," let the strip go.

5. The strip moves quickly up and down. Each time it moves down, it makes one vibration. Have your partner time 10 seconds. Count the number of vibrations. When your partner says "Stop," record the number of vibrations in the chart on the next page.

6. Repeat Steps 4 and 5 two more times.

7. Find the average number of vibrations of the three trials.

8. Now attach the small rock to the end of the strip. Repeat Steps 3–7.

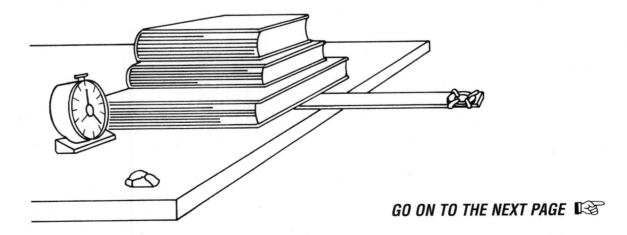

GO ON TO THE NEXT PAGE ☞

Name _____ Date _____

How Can You Compare the Inertia of Two Objects?, p. 2

INERTIA COMPARISON

Metal Strip with Washer	Vibrations per 10 Seconds	Metal Strip with Rock	Vibrations per 10 Seconds
Trial 1		Trial 1	
Trial 2		Trial 2	
Trial 3		Trial 3	
Total		Total	
Average		Average	

Answer the questions.

1. What was the average number of vibrations for the strip with the washer?

_____

_____

2. What was the average number of vibrations for the strip with the rock?

_____

_____

3. Was it easier for the strip to move the washer or the rock? Why?

_____

_____

4. Which object had greater inertia? Why?

_____

_____

5. Which object had greater mass? Why?

_____

_____

Accelerometer

The rate of change in velocity, or change in velocity over time, is called **acceleration**. Whether an object is speeding up, slowing down, or changing direction, it is accelerating. When an object slows down, or the velocity decreases, we sometimes say the object is decelerating. However, in scientific language, any change in velocity is called acceleration.

A force is a push or pull. When a force pushes or pulls an object in the opposite direction, there is negative acceleration. If it moves in the same direction, there is positive acceleration. Find out about acceleration in this activity.

You will need

☆ clear plastic bottle with cap

☆ water

☆ small piece of bar soap

1. Fill the bottle with water, leaving enough space for a small air bubble. Add the piece of bar soap so that the bubble will not attach to the wall of the bottle.

2. Screw the cap on the bottle. Set the bottle on its side on a table. The bubble should move to the center of the side that is up.

3. Pick up the bottle. Quickly push the bottle forward. What happened to the bubble?

4. Pull the bottle quickly back toward you. What happened to the bubble?

5. Carry the bottle as you walk in a straight path, then turn left and continue to walk in a straight path. What happened to the bubble?

Answer the questions.

1. What kinds of movement made the bubble move?

_____

_____

2. How are velocity and acceleration related?

_____

_____

Name _____   Date _____

How Does Mass Affect Acceleration?

Newton's *second law of motion* states that an object accelerates faster as the force gets larger or as the mass of the object gets smaller. Do this activity to see if Newton was correct.

You will need

⭐ 3 Styrofoam cups   ⭐ pin   ⭐ toy truck   ⭐ sand   ⭐ scissors
⭐ masking tape   ⭐ string   ⭐ pennies   ⭐ water   ⭐ ruler

1. Label the cups **A**, **B**, and **C**.

2. Punch a hole in the bottom of cup C using the pin. Make a pencil mark 1.5 cm up from the bottom of the cup on the inside. Tape the cup to the back of the toy truck.

3. Fill cup B with sand. Put the cup in the back of the truck.

4. Place the truck at one end of a table. Tie one end of the string to the front of the truck. Tie the other end through cup A.

5. Extend the string the length of the table. Let the string and cup A drop 30 cm over the edge of the table.

6. Drop some pennies into cup A until the truck moves.

7. Move the truck back to the starting point. Fill cup C with water up to the pencil mark. Let the truck go. Measure the distance between the drops of water that fall to the table from the hole in the bottom of the cup. Record it in the chart.

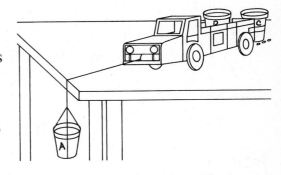

8. Return the truck to the starting point. Untape cup C from the truck, empty the cup, and retape it to the back of the truck. Dry the top of the table.

9. Remove the pennies from cup A. Be sure the empty cup still hangs over the edge of the table.

10. Remove the sand-filled cup B from the truck. Repeat Steps 6 and 7.

MEASURING ACCELERATION

Truck	Distance Between Drops
With Sand	
Without Sand	

📦 **Answer these questions on another piece of paper.**

1. What part of the experiment is the force?
2. What was the distance between the drops of water that fell from the truck carrying sand?
3. What was the distance between the drops of water that fell from the truck without sand?
4. Did the truck accelerate faster with the sand or without the sand? How do you know?
5. What caused the difference in acceleration?

Static Electricity

Have you ever rubbed a balloon on your shirt or your hair and then put it on the wall? Why does it stick? The reason is because of electric charges. Every object has electric charges, but they are too small to see. There are two kinds of charges: positive charges and negative charges. Objects that have more negative charges than positive charges are negatively charged. Objects that have more positive charges than negative charges are positively charged.

All matter contains a positive or negative charge. Negative charges can move from one object to another. **Static electricity** results when an object gains or loses a charge. The objects may attract or repel each other. If they attract, they pull together. If they repel, they push apart. Objects with like charges repel each other, while those with opposite charges attract each other.

Positively charged objects attract negatively charged objects and repel other positively charged objects. Negatively charged objects attract positively charged objects and repel other negatively charged objects.

⬚ **Darken the letter of the answer that best completes each sentence.**

1. If you rub a balloon on your shirt or in your hair and then touch it to the wall, it will _____.
   - Ⓐ stick to the wall
   - Ⓑ fall to the floor
   - Ⓒ roll up to the ceiling
   - Ⓓ push away from the wall

2. If pieces of confetti will stick to a balloon, then you know that the balloon is _____.
   - Ⓐ sticky
   - Ⓑ charged
   - Ⓒ uncharged
   - Ⓓ filled with helium

3. An object that has more negative charges than positive charges is _____.
   - Ⓐ uncharged
   - Ⓑ neutral
   - Ⓒ positively charged
   - Ⓓ negatively charged

4. If two balloons are both negatively charged, they will _____.
   - Ⓐ attract each other
   - Ⓑ repel each other
   - Ⓒ stick to each other
   - Ⓓ be neutral

Circuits

Electric charges do not always stay in one place. In fact, they can move very well through some materials. For example, you can use copper wires to connect a light bulb to a battery so that charges flow out of one end of the battery, through the light bulb, and into the other end of the battery. The loop made by the battery, wires, and light bulb is called a **circuit**. The flow of charges through the circuit is called **current electricity**. When the circuit is complete, or closed, the charges can travel all the way through it and will light the bulb. If the circuit is incomplete, or open, then the bulb will not light. A switch can be added to open and close the circuit so the light bulb can be turned on and off.

There is only one way to wire a circuit with just one light bulb and one battery. But if you add another light bulb, there are two ways to wire them together. In a **series circuit**, all of the electric charges travel first through one of the light bulbs and then through the other one. In a **parallel circuit**, there are two paths for the charges to follow. Some travel through one path to one of the light bulbs, while the rest travel through the other path to the other light bulb.

Darken the letter of the best answer.

1. Electric charges do not flow all the way through _____.
   Ⓐ an open circuit
   Ⓑ a closed circuit
   Ⓒ a wire
   Ⓓ a battery

2. If you remove the bulb from a circuit, the current will _____.
   Ⓐ get brighter
   Ⓑ get faster
   Ⓒ get dimmer
   Ⓓ stop flowing

3. Which part is not needed for a circuit to work?
   Ⓐ wires
   Ⓑ switch
   Ⓒ battery
   Ⓓ light bulb

Making an Electric Switch

When a **switch** is closed (or on), a circuit is completed. Electric current can pass through. When a switch is open (or off), the circuit is broken and the electric current cannot flow. Do this activity to learn more about how a switch works.

You will need

- ☆ 2 steel thumbtacks
- ☆ 1.5 volt dry cell
- ☆ 3 strips of insulated wire
- ☆ light bulb and bulb holder
- ☆ piece of wood, 12 cm x 8 cm
- ☆ tin snips
- ☆ wire cutters
- ☆ tin can
- ☆ hammer
- ☆ metric ruler

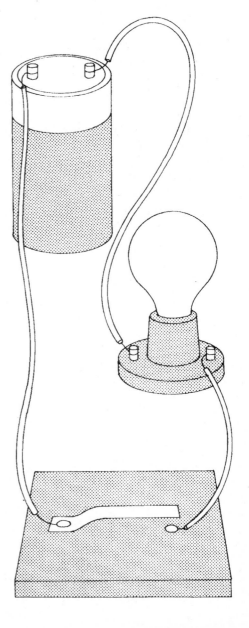

1. Strip about 1 cm of insulation from the ends of all the wires.

2. Have your teacher cut a 6 cm x 2 cm strip of metal from the tin can and bend it to form an S.

   CAUTION: Be careful when handling the metal strip. The edges may be sharp.

3. Connect two wires to the bulb holder. Make a loop at the end of one of these wires. Place a tack through the loop and hammer it into the wood.

4. Attach the other wire from the bulb holder to one terminal of the dry cell.

5. Loop one end of the remaining wire around the second tack. Hammer the tack through one end of the metal strip and into the wood. It should be placed about 4 cm from the first tack.

6. Connect the other end of the remaining wire to the dry cell. To complete the circuit, turn on your switch. Just press down on the metal strip. Be sure the strip touches the tack.

   What happens? _____

Is It a Conductor or an Insulator?

A **conductor** is a material that allows a current to flow through it easily, such as metal. An **insulator** is a material that keeps a current from moving through it, such as rubber or plastic. This activity shows you more about conductors and insulators.

You will need

- ☆ 3 pieces of insulated copper wire, each 30 cm long and stripped back 2.5 cm on each end
- ☆ light bulb in socket
- ☆ sheet of aluminum foil
- ☆ pencil
- ☆ D-size battery
- ☆ screwdriver
- ☆ door key
- ☆ sheet of paper
- ☆ penny
- ☆ rubber band

1. Look at the chart on the next page. Read the list of objects in the *Item Tested* column. Predict which items are insulators and which are conductors. Record your predictions.

2. Connect the three pieces of wire, light bulb, and battery as shown in the picture.

3. Hold the uncovered ends of the two wires to the foil. Watch what happens.

4. Record your observation in the chart on the next page.

5. Repeat Steps 3 and 4 for each item listed in the chart.

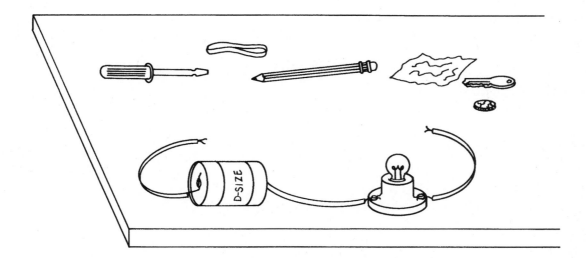

GO ON TO THE NEXT PAGE ☞

Is It a Conductor or an Insulator?, p. 2

Item Tested	Prediction	Conductor	Insulator
Aluminum foil			
Door key			
Paper			
Penny			
Rubber band			
Pencil			

  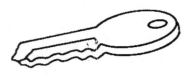

Answer the questions.

1. Which items were conductors?

   _____

   _____

2. Which items were insulators?

   _____

   _____

3. Which of your predictions were correct? Which were not correct?

   _____

   _____

4. What kinds of materials make good conductors?

   _____

   _____

How Can You Make a Series Circuit?

A **resistor** is a device that uses electrical energy because it resists the flow of energy. A light bulb is an example of a resistor. When a circuit has two or more resistors and the electrical current flows in one direction, then it is called a **series circuit**. In this kind of circuit, the flow of electricity stays the same. The resistors must share the flow, so they may not be able to work to full capacity. You will make a series circuit in this activity.

You will need

- ☆ 4 pieces of insulated copper wire, each 30 cm long and stripped back 2.5 cm on each end
- ☆ 2 light bulbs in sockets
- ☆ 1.5 volt dry cell
- ☆ switch
- ☆ screwdriver

1. Create a series circuit with wires as follows:
   - join one terminal of the dry cell to one light bulb
   - join the first light bulb to the second one
   - join the second light bulb to the switch
   - join the switch to the remaining dry cell terminal.

2. Close the switch, then open it. What happened?

3. Unscrew one light bulb. What do you think will happen when you close the switch?

4. Close the switch, then open it. What happened?

Answer these questions on another piece of paper.

1. What happened when you closed the switch the first time?
2. What happened when you closed the switch after you unscrewed one light bulb?
3. Through how many paths can an electric current flow in a series circuit? How do you know?
4. Write two hypotheses for this activity. Each one should begin with the word *If* and have the word *then* in it.

How Can You Make a Parallel Circuit?

A **parallel circuit** has more than one path that an electric current can travel through. These circuits usually have a fuse or circuit breaker joined to them to keep the wires from getting too hot. You will make a parallel circuit in this activity.

You will need

- ☆ 7 pieces of insulated copper wire, each 30 cm long and stripped back 2.5 cm on each end
- ☆ 3 light bulbs in sockets
- ☆ 1.5 volt dry cell
- ☆ switch
- ☆ screwdriver

1. Create a parallel circuit with wires as follows:
   - join one terminal of the dry cell to one light bulb
   - join the first light bulb to the second bulb
   - join the second light bulb to the third bulb
   - join the bulbs in the reverse order to the switch
   - join the switch to the remaining dry cell terminal.

2. Close the switch, then open it. What happened?

3. Unscrew one light bulb. What do you think will happen when you close the switch?

4. Close the switch, then open it. What happened?

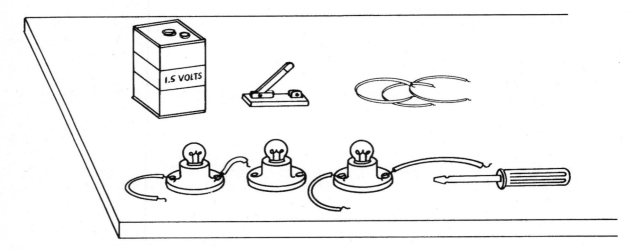

📦 **Answer these questions on another piece of paper.**

1. What happened when you closed the switch the first time?
2. What happened when you closed the switch the second time?
3. Through how many paths can an electric current flow in a parallel circuit? How do you know?
4. What is the difference between a series circuit and a parallel circuit?

Circuit Diagrams

Engineers use symbols when they design circuits. The chart shows some of those symbols.

 **In each space below, draw a diagram of the circuit described using the symbols given on the chart. The first one is done for you.**

1. A series circuit with 1 dry cell, 2 light bulbs, and an open switch.

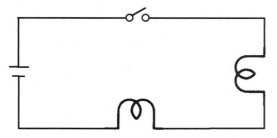

2. A parallel circuit with 2 dry cells, 3 light bulbs, and an open switch.

CHART OF ELECTRICAL SYMBOLS

CIRCUIT PART		SYMBOL
dry cell		
light bulb		
open switch		
closed switch		
wire		
fuse		
broken fuse		

3. A series circuit with 2 dry cells, 4 light bulbs, and a closed switch.

4. A parallel circuit with 1 dry cell, 2 light bulbs, and an open switch.

Fuses

As electric current flows, wires and other objects in the circuit may get too hot. They can cause the circuit to short and change the flow of electricity. A **fuse** is made with a wire that melts if the current gets too hot. You will make a fuse in this activity.

You will need

☆ aluminum foil	☆ 2 dry cells	☆ 2 paper clips	☆ ruler
☆ wooden block	☆ scissors	☆ 2 thumbtacks	☆ wire
☆ screwdriver with insulated handle		☆ light bulb in socket	

Safety Tip: This activity must be supervised by an adult.

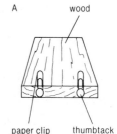

1. Place each paper clip against the underside of a thumbtack. Press the thumbtacks into the wooden block as shown. The paper clips should be about 3 cm apart and upright against the wood.

2. Place a strip of aluminum foil about 5 cm long by 1 cm wide between the clips.

3. Remove some insulation from two of the wires so that the circuit can be set up as shown in Figure B.

4. Set up the dry cells, wire, and bulb as shown.

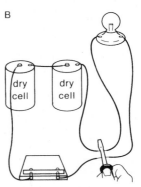

5. While holding the insulated handle of the screwdriver, carefully touch the metal to the two stripped wires. Observe what happens to the aluminum.

Answer the questions.

1. How did you short the circuit? _____

_____

2. Did the current travel back to the source through the bulb or the screwdriver?

_____

3. What happened to the foil? Why? _____

_____

4. Why is a fuse helpful in a circuit? _____

_____

_____

Making a Magnet

Magnets attract objects made of iron, nickel, and cobalt. The force of a magnet is strongest at its poles, or ends. Some metals can become like a magnet. You will make a magnet in this activity.

You will need

- ☆ bar magnet
- ☆ candle with holder
- ☆ hammer
- ☆ 3 iron nails
- ☆ matches
- ☆ paper clips
- ☆ pliers

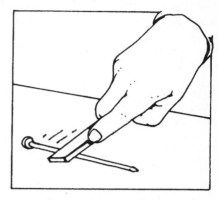

NOTE: This activity must be supervised by an adult.

1. Stroke one of the iron nails with the pole of the magnet in one direction only.

2. Try to pick up the paper clips with the nail.

3. Remove the clips. Then, hammer along the length of the nail several times. Try to pick up the clips again.

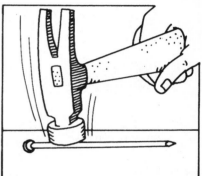

4. Repeat Steps 1–2 with another nail. Remove the clips.

5. Stroke the nail with the pole of the magnet in both directions. Try to pick up the clips again.

6. Repeat Steps 1–2 with another nail. Then, remove the clips.

7. Hold the nail with the pliers and place the nail in the flame of a candle for about three minutes. Try to pick up the clips again.

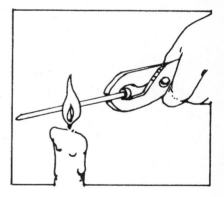

 Answer these questions on another piece of paper.

1. How did you make the nails act like magnets?
2. What happened to the nails after you hammered or heated them?
3. What happened to the nail after rubbing it with the magnet in both directions?
4. What are three ways in which magnetism can be destroyed?

Magnetic Force

Each end of a magnet is called a **pole**. There is a north pole, labeled *N*, and a south pole, labeled *S*. The magnetic force is strongest at the poles. The poles have different forces. If you put the ends of the poles of two magnets close to each other, the magnets will either push away from each other or pull toward each other. If the magnets pull together, the poles are unlike poles. If they push apart, the poles are like poles.

Below are drawings of magnets. On each, draw the lines of force that show the location of the magnetic field.

1.

N	S

2.

S	N		N	S

3.

S	N		S	N

Answer the questions.

4. What do the letters *N* and *S* stand for on the magnets?

_____

5. How could you test the accuracy of the drawings you made in questions 1–3?

_____

_____

_____

_____

_____

_____

_____

How Can You See the Effect of a Magnetic Field?

The space around the magnet is the **magnetic field**. The force is strongest around the poles of the magnets. Do this activity to see the effect of a magnetic force.

You will need

★ metal filings (or a steel wool pad cut into small pieces)

★ bar magnet   ★ plastic cup   ★ sheet of plastic

1. Place the bar magnet on the table. Cover it with the sheet of plastic.

2. Sprinkle the iron filings on the plastic sheet on the magnet.

3. Gently tap the edge of the sheet.

4. Draw what you see in the space below.

Answer the questions.

1. What is a magnetic field? _____

_____

2. What parts of the magnet have the strongest magnetic field?

_____

_____

How Do Nonmagnetic Materials Affect a Magnet?

Materials made of metal, such as iron, nickel, and cobalt, are attracted by a magnet. In this activity, you will find out if nonmagnetic materials affect a magnetic field.

You will need

- ★ alnico magnet
- ★ aluminum foil
- ★ block of wood
- ★ cloth
- ★ waxed paper
- ★ a paper clip
- ★ squares of paper
- ★ iron nail
- ★ string 37 cm (15 in.) long
- ★ ring stand with test-tube holder

1. Set up the materials as shown in the drawing.

2. Pass the squares of paper through the space between the clip and the pole of the magnet. Record your results in the chart.

3. Pass the foil, cloth, waxed paper, and nail through the space.

4. Repeat the experiment with the poles reversed.

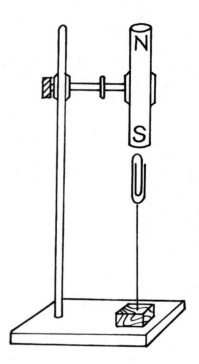

 Answer the questions.

1. Why is the paper clip held in place? _____

   _____

2. What happened in Step 2? Explain. _____

   _____

3. Did any of the materials affect the magnetic field?

   Why? _____

   _____

4. What happened when you reversed the bar magnet so the N pole pointed down? Explain. _____

   _____

MAGNETIC ATTRACTION	
Material	**Effect**
paper	
foil	
cloth	
waxed paper	
nail	

Electromagnets

Electromagnets are made by wrapping wire around a long piece of iron. An electric current travels through the wire and causes the iron to become magnetized. The iron loses its magnetic force when the current is turned off. The magnetic field is stronger when more wire is wrapped around the metal or a stronger current travels through the wire.

a.
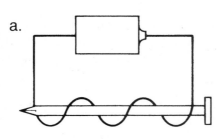

b.
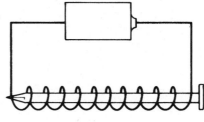

c.
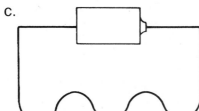

d.
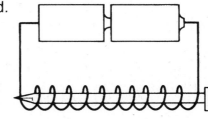
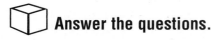

Answer the questions.

1. Arrange the letters of the electromagnets in order of increasing strength.

   _____

2. Many devices, such as telephones and cranes that move metal, use electromagnets. Choose a device and research to find how it uses an electromagnet. Write a brief explanation below.

   _____

   _____

   _____

   _____

   _____

   _____

   _____

   _____

Unit 2: Earth and Space Science

BACKGROUND INFORMATION

The Earth is made up of three materials: solids, liquids, and gases. The solids inside the Earth are such things as minerals, rocks, and soil. The liquid with which we are most familiar is water. But the Earth also has liquid metal and rock under its surface. And various gases, mostly oxygen and nitrogen, make up the atmosphere that allows life on the Earth.

The Earth

The Earth has a diameter of about 8,000 miles (12,900 km) and a circumference of about 25,000 miles (40,250 km). The Earth is made up of three layers. The outer layer of the Earth, called the crust, is quite thin, ranging from 3 to 34 miles (5–55 km) thick. We live on the crust, and most of the rocks and minerals we recognize come from the crust.

Below the crust is the mantle. The mantle is about 1,800 miles (2,900 km) thick, and it is made of mostly solid rock. The mantle is very hot, up to 5,400° F (3,000° C). Below the mantle is the core. The core is about 2,200 miles (3,500 km) thick, and it has a temperature as high as 7,200° F (4,000° C). Most scientists think the core has two parts, an outer core and an inner core. The outer core is made of melted iron and nickel. The inner core is a solid ball of iron and nickel.

Minerals and Rocks

Rocks are made up of minerals. Minerals have four characteristics that classify them as minerals. 1. They are substances that occur naturally. 2. They are inorganic solids. 3. Minerals of the same type usually have the same chemical composition. 4. The atoms of minerals are arranged in a regular pattern that forms crystals.

Rocks are classified into three basic groups: igneous, sedimentary, and metamorphic. These groups are based on how the rock is formed.

Igneous rocks begin as molten rock, a red-hot liquid. *Igneous* means "fire," so igneous rocks can be called "fire rocks." After a long while, the molten rock cools and hardens to form solid rock. The hardening can occur on the surface or below the surface of the Earth. Molten rock that is on the surface of the Earth is called lava. Granite is an example of igneous rock.

Sedimentary rocks are made up of sediments, or bits of rock and sand. The sediments piled up to form layers. The weight of the layers squeezed the sediments. Chemicals in the sediments cemented them together. The squeezing and cementing eventually caused the sediments to harden into layers of rock. Sandstone is an example of sedimentary rock.

Sometimes rocks that have already formed become buried deep in the Earth. There, great pressures inside the Earth squeeze the rocks. Great heat makes the rocks very hot, but does not melt them. The squeezing and heat slowly change these rocks from one kind to another. The new kind of rock is called a metamorphic rock. *Metamorphic* means "changed." Igneous, sedimentary, and even other metamorphic rocks can be changed to form new metamorphic rocks. Slate is an example of metamorphic rock. Slate is formed from the sedimentary rock shale.

Soil

Soil is the grainy material that covers much of the land on the Earth. Soil is made of tiny bits of rock, minerals, organic materials, water, and air. Soil is needed for life to exist on the Earth. Plants need soil to grow. Then, animals, including people, eat the plants to stay alive. Soil is created through a long process. Rocks break down through weathering and erosion into a stony product called parent soil. This type of soil is broken down further, mostly through weathering. Organic matter called humus mixes with the parent soil. When the long process is complete, the rock bits and humus have mixed to produce fertile soil, which is good for growing plants.

Weathering and Erosion

Any process that causes rocks or landforms to break down is called weathering. Weathering is caused by several agents, including water, wind, ice, and plants. Weathering is usually a slow process, causing the gradual deterioration of the rocks or landforms.

Erosion is another way in which rocks and landforms are broken down or worn away. Erosion is the process in which weathered rock and soil are moved from one place to another. The most effective agents of erosion are moving water, waves, gravity, wind, and glaciers.

Earthquakes and Volcanoes

A much more violent process can change the landscape in only a few minutes. These rapid changes are produced by the actions of earthquakes and volcanoes. Earthquakes and volcanoes can change the landscape quickly, and they can also cause great damage to property and human life. Earthquakes can cause great splits in the ground, or large sections of the Earth can be pushed upward. Buildings can be damaged or even knocked down by the shaking that earthquakes cause. The lava flow of a volcano can damage the area around the volcano. The volcano's ash cloud can cause health hazards for people, and it can even alter the weather. Sometimes volcanoes explode. When this happens, everything nearby is flattened or burned.

To understand earthquakes and volcanoes, you must understand the structure of the Earth's crust. Scientists now believe that the Earth's crust is broken into about ten pieces, called plates. These plates move. Scientists believe that at one time in the very distant past, all the continents were joined. The continents were on some of these plates. Over time, the plates moved apart, causing the continents to move apart, or drift. A look at a world map will show how this theory is possible.

Scientists believe the plates can move in three ways. These movements occur at the boundary lines between the plates. These boundary lines are called faults. When two plates push against each other, they collide. The thin part of one plate slowly pushes its way under the thick part of another plate. The upper plate then rises. This is how some mountains are formed. Earthquakes are also common where plates collide

Two plates can move apart, causing magma (molten rock) to squeeze up between the plates. The magma then cools and hardens into new crust. Volcanoes and earthquakes are very common where plates move apart.

Two plates can also slide past each other, causing a great grinding. The San Andreas Fault in California divides two plates. One is called the North American Plate, and the other is the Pacific Plate. These two plates slide against each other often, so that earthquakes are common in California.

Water

Water is our most precious resource. Water covers about 70 percent of the Earth's surface. Without water, life could not exist. Our bodies are about 65 percent water. We use water in many ways. Water is an amazing substance, too. It can be a solid, a liquid, and a gas. It can change from a solid state (ice) to a liquid state (water) to a gaseous state (water vapor) and back again.

The Water Cycle

Water often changes from its liquid form to its gaseous form and back to its liquid form in a process called the water cycle. The three main steps in the water cycle are evaporation, condensation, and precipitation. Evaporation is necessary to get the liquid water into its gaseous form of water vapor in the air. Condensation is needed to turn the vapor back to a liquid in the clouds. And precipitation returns the liquid water to the Earth.

Evaporation occurs as liquid water is heated and changed into water vapor. The water vapor is then carried up into the sky by rising air. Condensation takes place as the rising water vapor cools and is changed into liquid water, forming clouds. Precipitation happens as water droplets grow heavy and fall to the Earth as rain, snow, or some other type of precipitation.

Gases and the Atmosphere

We live on the crust of the Earth. We have food and water. But another part of the Earth's structure is necessary to sustain life. That part is called the atmosphere. The atmosphere is made up of various gases, mostly nitrogen and oxygen, that allow us to survive on the Earth. The atmosphere is about 500 miles (800 km) high, and it is held in place by the Earth's gravity.

The atmosphere has four layers. Closest to the Earth is the troposphere, the layer in which we live. The troposphere is only a thin band, about 5 to 10 miles (8–16 km) thick. All the Earth's weather occurs in the troposphere. The troposphere also contains the air we need to live. The air in the troposphere is about 80 percent nitrogen and 20 percent oxygen. There are also small amounts of other gases, including argon and carbon dioxide.

Above the troposphere is the stratosphere, a layer that is from about 5 to 50 miles (8–80 km) high. The stratosphere has only a few clouds, which are mostly made of ice crystals. In the stratosphere are the fast moving winds known as the jet stream. The air in the lower part of the stratosphere is cold. In the upper part of the stratosphere, the temperature increases. The important ozone layer is in the upper stratosphere. The ozone absorbs ultraviolet energy from the Sun, which causes the temperature there to rise. The ozone layer is important because it protects creatures on the Earth from the harmful ultraviolet rays.

Above the stratosphere is the ionosphere, which stretches from about 50 miles to about 300 miles (80–500 km) above the Earth. There is almost no air in the ionosphere. But the ionosphere is useful for radio astronomy and communication with satellites. The natural displays of light called auroras occur in the ionosphere.

The top layer of the atmosphere is called the exosphere. It begins about 300 miles (500 km) above the Earth, but it has no definite top boundary. This layer is the beginning of what we call outer space. The exosphere contains mostly oxygen and helium gases. This layer also has a very high temperature, up to several thousand degrees.

Weather

Weather, in its most basic explanation, is caused by the uneven heating of the Earth's surface by the Sun. The land and the water are heated differently. This uneven heating causes pockets of air with different temperatures. Cool air is heavier than warm air. As a result, the cooler air moves under the warmer air, so the lighter warm air is pushed up. This movement of air causes winds. These factors all work together to produce weather.

As you recall, we live in the layer of the Earth's atmosphere called the troposphere. Air in the troposphere moves constantly. The air is heated, not directly by the Sun, but by the air's contact with the Earth. Air closer to the Earth is warmer than air higher up. Cold air is heavier than warm air, so the cold air moves downward. The warm air rises as it is displaced, setting up the patterns of air circulation in the troposphere.

Near the Earth's surface, the sinking air results in high-pressure zones, called ridges. The rising air results in low-pressure zones, called troughs. The differences in air pressure produce winds. Wind moves out of high-pressure zones in a clockwise direction and into low-pressure zones in a counterclockwise direction. Weather data identifies winds by the direction from which they come. For example, a wind moving toward the south is called a north wind, because north is the direction from which it comes.

Great air masses move slowly across the Earth's surface. These moving air masses take on the characteristics of the surface beneath them. Air moving over a warm surface is warmed, and air moving over a cold surface is cooled. Air moving over water becomes moist, and air moving over land becomes drier. As it moves, the air mass causes changes in the weather of an area.

Precipitation

Precipitation is one of the most obvious features of weather. As you recall, precipitation is the third step in the water cycle, following evaporation and condensation. Sometimes precipitation does not fall in an area for a long period of time. Plants and crops can die, and sometimes even animals and people die as a result of the lack of water. When an area does not receive precipitation for a long time, it is said to be in a drought.

Clouds

Another of the most obvious, and sometimes most spectacular, features of weather is the cloud. Clouds can take several forms, from thin and wispy to dense and billowy. How do clouds form? Remember the movement of air, with warm air rising as the cold air sinks? First, through evaporation, water on the Earth's surface becomes water vapor in the air. As the warm air rises and expands, it naturally begins to cool. Water vapor in the air starts to condense around tiny particles in the air, such as dust or smoke, forming droplets. Clouds form in different shapes, depending on their height, the coolness of the air, and the amount of water vapor in the air.

The water droplets grow bigger as more water vapor condenses. When the droplets get so large they cannot be held up by the rising air, they fall as rain or some other form of precipitation. If the cloud is cold and contains crystals of ice, snow may fall instead of rain.

There are three main types of clouds: cirrus, cumulus, and stratus. Cirrus clouds are high above the Earth and are usually seen in fair weather. These clouds, made of ice crystals, are wispy and streak the sky. Cumulus clouds are white and fluffy, looking much like cotton balls. They are often seen in good weather,

though they can produce rain showers or snow. Stratus clouds are low, dark clouds close to the Earth. They often produce rain or snow.

Stormy Weather

Weather comes in many forms, fair and foul. Fair weather includes sunny days, gentle breezes, and mild temperatures. But foul weather is more spectacular, accompanied as it often is by powerful displays of wind, rain, lightning, and thunder. One of the most common examples of foul weather is the thunderstorm. Approaching thunderstorms are often accompanied by towering cumulus clouds called thunderheads. These billowy clouds have flat tops and dark bottoms. Thunderheads are formed when warm, moist air rises. As the rising air begins to cool, water vapor in the air condenses, and cumulus clouds form. The hot ground causes the heated air to rise faster and higher. The cumulus clouds grow larger and taller, often reaching ten miles or more into the air. As the clouds grow in size, they become more likely to produce rain.

Thunderheads also produce two well-known features of stormy weather: lightning and thunder. Lightning is an electrical spark caused by friction inside the thunderhead. As the clouds grow, raindrops scrape against each other, and friction is produced. This friction builds up an electrical charge, just as you do when you scrape your feet across a carpet. Most of the electric charges in the lower part of the cloud are negative. These negative charges emit a spark that jumps toward a positive charge on the ground. This spark is what we call lightning. The lightning instantly heats the air around its path. This heated air expands quickly and collides with cooler air. The collision between the heated air and the cooler air produces the sound we know as thunder.

Climate

Weather is a short-term atmospheric event. The average weather of a particular place over a long period of time is known as climate. The climate of an area is determined by the air masses associated with that area's location on the Earth's surface. Warm air masses near the Equator make the climate there tropical. Cold air masses make the climate around the poles polar.

Local weather conditions can produce situations called microclimates, in which the climate of one location differs from the climates of surrounding areas. Mountain shadows or bodies of water can alter local climates. Human activity can also alter local climates. The greenhouse effect is a condition in which carbon dioxide gases trap radiated heat from the Earth's surface. This trapped heat causes temperatures to rise. A prolonged greenhouse effect could lead to global warming, a permanent change in the Earth's climates.

The Sun

Life on the Earth begins with the Sun, and the Earth's weather is also caused by the Sun and its energy. The Sun produces energy in the form of heat and light. In the center of the Sun, its core, nuclear fusion reactions change hydrogen into helium. These reactions release an unbelievable amount of energy. At the core, the Sun burns at a temperature of about 27 million degrees F (15 million degrees C). The energy moves from the core to the surface of the Sun, which has a temperature of almost 4 million degrees F (2.2 million degrees C). The energy then travels through space as electromagnetic waves of light and heat.

The Earth is 93 million miles (150 million km) from the Sun, so only a tiny amount of the Sun's energy reaches the Earth. But this small amount is enough to sustain life and create weather on the Earth. Much of the Sun's energy and harmful rays are filtered out by the Earth's atmosphere. About half of the Sun's energy is absorbed or reflected by the ozone, clouds, or the air. About 50 percent is absorbed by the Earth's surface.

The Sun is much larger than the Earth, with a diameter of about 840,000 miles (1,352,400 km), compared to the Earth's diameter of about 8,000 miles (12,900 km). But the Sun is, in fact, only a medium-sized star. Many early people believed that the Sun moved around the Earth, but the opposite is true. The Earth orbits around the Sun, once every 365 days or 1 year.

The Solar System

The Earth joins eight other planets in the solar system. These nine planets orbit around the Sun. (Recent research by astronomers suggests there may be a tenth planet somewhere beyond Pluto.) They all receive energy from the Sun, but they receive varying amounts based on their distance from the Sun. The inner planets (Mercury, Venus, Earth, Mars) receive more energy because they are closer. The outer planets (Jupiter, Saturn, Uranus, Neptune, Pluto) are very cold planets where the chance of life is very small. Students can remember the order of the planets outward from the Sun by using this saying: "My Very Energetic Mother Just Sent Us Nine Pizzas."

The other planets are mostly quite different from the Earth. The planet closest to the Sun, Mercury, has a year, or one orbit of the Sun, that is only 88 Earth days long. On Mercury, the surface temperature can be as low as about –290° F (–173° C) or as high as 800 °F (500 °C). For the most distant planet, Pluto, one orbit takes 248 Earth years. Pluto is about three billion miles (4.8 billion km) from the Sun. On Neptune, winds sometimes blow up to 700 miles per hour (1,125 km/hour).

The planets are held in their orbits by the Sun's gravitational pull. Likewise, the Earth and the farther planets have smaller bodies, or moons, that orbit around them, held by each planet's gravitational pull. The Earth has one moon. On the other hand, Jupiter has at least 17 moons.

The Moon

The Moon is a satellite of the Earth. It is about one fourth the size of the Earth, with a diameter of about 2,100 miles (3,400 km). The Moon appears about the same size as the Sun in the sky, but that is only because the Moon is so much closer than the Sun. The Moon is about

240,000 miles (384,000 km) from the Earth, and the Sun is about 93 million miles (150 million km). The Moon orbits the Earth once about every 28 days.

The Moon has no light of its own, but it seems to shine because it reflects the Sun's light. The Moon also has no atmosphere and no life. The Moon's gravity is only about one sixth as strong as the Earth's gravity. A person who weighs 60 pounds (27 kg) on the Earth would weigh only 10 pounds (4.5 kg) on the Moon!

Stars

Stars are great balls of gas that burn at tremendous temperatures. They undergo a nuclear fusion reaction that changes hydrogen to helium. Our Sun is the nearest star. Most stars are very, very far away. Stars are very, very bright, but they seem dim to us because of their great distance, like a burning match many miles away. Stars are so far away from the Earth that their distances are measured in light-years. A light-year is the distance light moving at 186,000 miles per second (300,000 km/sec) travels in one year. Stars differ from one another in their color, brightness (or magnitude), and size. Stars are classified by these attributes. One of the brighter stars seen from the Earth is Polaris, also known as the North Star.

Some stars appear grouped in recognizable shapes. These groups are called constellations. Most constellations were named by ancient people. Some constellations are Orion, Leo, Scorpius, and Ursa Major, also called the Great Bear. The Big Dipper is part of Ursa Major. Constellations are noted on star charts, which are like maps of the sky. On a clear night, about 6,000 stars are visible to the unaided eye.

A larger grouping of stars is called a galaxy. Galaxies contain billions of stars, and there are billions of galaxies in the universe. Our solar system is in the Milky Way Galaxy. On a clear, dark night, away from city lights, the Milky Way is visible as a sparkling band across the vault of the sky.

Changes in the Sky

Changes in the sky occur on a regular basis. The stars slowly shift their positions in the sky, seeming to rise in the east and move across the sky to set in the west. Some stars are constant and are always visible in the night sky. These are called circumpolar stars. The Sun moves from east to west on its journey through the day. The Moon, too, moves across the sky each night and also through its phases. The Earth itself moves as it revolves around the Sun, and it also tilts as it rotates on its axis.

The Movement of the Earth

The Earth moves constantly, rotating on its axis, which causes the day and night cycle. The Earth also revolves around the Sun and tilts on its axis. As the tilt changes, parts of the Earth are closer to the Sun. The seasons occur as a result of the Earth's tilt on its axis. During the six months that the North Pole is tilted toward the Sun, the Northern Hemisphere gets more sunlight than the Southern Hemisphere does. The atmosphere then is warmer in the Northern Hemisphere, resulting in warmer weather. During the time the North Pole is tilted toward the Sun, the Northern Hemisphere experiences late spring, summer, and early fall. At the same time, the Southern Hemisphere is having late fall, winter, and early spring. The Northern Hemisphere experiences these later seasons when the North Pole is tilted away from the Sun.

The summer and winter solstices occur in late June and December each year. The summer solstice is the day your hemisphere of the Earth is tilted most toward the Sun. This day has the greatest number of hours of daylight. The winter solstice is the day your hemisphere is tilted most away from the Sun. This day has the fewest hours of daylight.

The spring (vernal) and fall (autumnal) equinoxes occur in late March and September each year. At the time of these two equinoxes, the Sun is directly above the Equator, and each hemisphere of the Earth receives equal numbers of hours of sunlight and darkness.

Studying the Skies

A place that gives shows about the stars and planets is called a planetarium. You can make a simple planetarium with a flashlight and an oatmeal box or frozen juice can. Carefully punch the shape of a constellation in the end of the box or can. Then, in a dark room, shine the flashlight inside the box or can and project the constellation on the wall or ceiling.

Scientists who study the sky and its objects are called astronomers. Astronomers use telescopes and radio waves to study the galaxies and the universe. Astronomers work in places called observatories. Two famous observatories are Palomar Observatory in California and McDonald Observatory in Texas. Astronomers can also use the Hubble Space Telescope to see even farther into space.

RELATED READING

- *Asteroids, Comets, and Meteors: The Milky Way and Other Galaxies* by Gregory Vogt (Millbrook Press, 1996).

- *The Big Rivers: The Missouri, the Mississippi, and the Ohio* by Bruce Hiscock (Atheneum, 1997).

- *Blizzard! The Storm That Changed America* by Jim Murphy (Scholastic Press, 2000).

- *Earth's Fiery Fury* by Sandra Downs (Twenty-First Century Books, 2000).

- *Exploring the Earth with John Wesley Powell* by Michael Elsohn Ross (Carolrhoda Books, 2000).

- *The Kingfisher Young People's Book of Oceans* by David Lambert (Kingfisher, 1997).

- *The Kingfisher Young People's Book of Space* by Martin Redfern (Kingfisher, 1998).

- *Nature on the Rampage Series* (Steadwell Books, 2000 and 2002).

- *Our Universe Series* by Gregory Vogt (Raintree Steck-Vaughn, 2001).

- *Restless Planet Series* (Raintree Steck-Vaughn, 2000).

- *Sunburns, Twisters, and Thunderclaps: The Science of Weather* by Janice Parker (Science at Work Series, Raintree Steck-Vaughn, 2000).

Unit 2 Assessment

Read each statement. Write *T* on the line if the statement is true. Write *F* if the statement is false.

_____ **1.** The Earth's core is very cold.

_____ **2.** Weathering is the breaking down of rocks.

_____ **3.** Most of the water in the oceans is fresh water.

_____ **4.** The ocean floor is completely flat.

_____ **5.** All places on the Earth have the same weather at the same time.

_____ **6.** The atmosphere is made up of at least four layers.

_____ **7.** Precipitation can take the form of rain, hail, sleet, or snow.

_____ **8.** The spinning of the Earth on its axis is called rotation.

Darken the letter of the answer that best completes each sentence.

9. The mantle of the Earth is made of _____.
   Ⓐ mostly solid rock
   Ⓑ very cool rock
   Ⓒ dust
   Ⓓ nickel and iron

10. One theory says that all the continents were once joined in a great land mass called _____.
   Ⓐ Pandora
   Ⓑ Panorama
   Ⓒ Atlantis
   Ⓓ Pangea

11. An earthquake is _____.
   Ⓐ an opening in the Earth's crust through which lava escapes
   Ⓑ a sudden movement in the Earth's crust
   Ⓒ never the cause of much damage
   Ⓓ a kind of chemical

12. The water cycle is _____.
   Ⓐ the movement of water between the air and the ground
   Ⓑ a form of transportation
   Ⓒ a weather symbol
   Ⓓ an air mass

GO ON TO THE NEXT PAGE ☞

Unit 2 Assessment, p. 2

Darken the letter of the answer that best completes each sentence.

13. The three steps of the water cycle are
_____.
   Ⓐ igneous, sedimentary, and
   metamorphic
   Ⓑ troposphere, stratosphere, and
   ionosphere
   Ⓒ evaporation, condensation, and
   precipitation
   Ⓓ rain, snow, and fog

14. The change in water from a liquid to a
gas is called _____.
   Ⓐ condensation
   Ⓑ evaporation
   Ⓒ rain
   Ⓓ snow

15. Water vapor changes into a liquid
when the air gets _____.
   Ⓐ wetter
   Ⓑ cooler
   Ⓒ warmer
   Ⓓ drier

16. Mountain chains on the oceans' floors
are called _____.
   Ⓐ the Rocky Mountains
   Ⓑ mid-ocean ridges
   Ⓒ trenches
   Ⓓ the continental shelf

17. The two main gases in the Earth's
atmosphere are nitrogen and _____.
   Ⓐ oxygen
   Ⓑ water vapor
   Ⓒ carbon dioxide
   Ⓓ hydrogen

18. A storm in the shape of a funnel with
high winds is a _____.
   Ⓐ blizzard
   Ⓑ hurricane
   Ⓒ thunderstorm
   Ⓓ tornado

19. The force that holds planets and moons
in orbit is called _____.
   Ⓐ space
   Ⓑ weight
   Ⓒ gravity
   Ⓓ rotation

20. The collection of soil and bits of rock
at the mouth of a river is called a
_____.
   Ⓐ comet
   Ⓑ delta
   Ⓒ alpha
   Ⓓ pond

Name _____ Date _____

Inside the Earth

The Earth is composed of layers. Many scientists believe that the Earth and its solar system formed billions of years ago from a huge cloud of dust. Over time, the cloud shrank. Parts of the cloud began spinning, eventually forming a star—the Sun—and nine hot planets revolving around the Sun. As they cooled, some of the planets, like Earth, developed rocky surfaces. Using instruments such as the seismograph, scientists have discovered that as Earth slowly cooled, it formed three layers: the crust, the mantle, and the core.

The thin, rocky surface layer is called the **crust**. Earth's crust is composed of various kinds of rocks, and it is not uniform in thickness; it is thicker under the continents than it is under the oceans. But the rock under the ocean floor is heavier than the rock under the continents. Earth's middle layer is called the **mantle**. The mantle is made of very heavy rocks and is subdivided into two areas, the upper mantle and the lower mantle. The rocks of the lower mantle are semisolid, like melted plastic. Below the mantle is the **core**. The core is also divided into two areas, the outer core and the inner core. The outer core is liquid, while the inner core is solid.

Complete these analogies.

1. The Earth's crust is to the shell of an egg as the Earth's _____ is to the white of an egg and as the Earth's _____ is to the yolk of an egg.

2. A _____ is to the study of the Earth as an X-ray machine is to the study of the human body.

3. Label this cross section of the Earth.

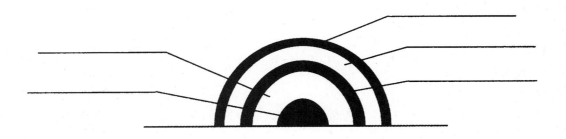

Answer these questions on another piece of paper.

4. How does rock under the continents differ from rock under the oceans?
5. How do upper-mantle rocks differ from lower-mantle rocks?
6. How does the outer core differ from the inner core?

Rocks

Rocks are all around you. They form the crust of the Earth itself. People use rocks for many things. They climb them, they collect them, they wear them, and they even build things with them. Rocks change. They break down, melt, change shape, harden, and soften. Rocks are found in three forms: igneous, metamorphic, and sedimentary.

Igneous rocks are formed when red-hot melted rock cools down. Where would you find red-hot melted rock? It is deep inside the Earth. Sometimes this melted rock comes to the surface as the lava that flows from volcanoes. Granite is a kind of igneous rock.

Sedimentary rocks are formed when tiny bits of rocks are worn away. The bits, called sediments, are washed away by rain and snow. The sediments settle in streams and river beds, as well as on the ocean floor. Over a long time, the sediments harden to form rock. An example of a sedimentary rock is sandstone.

Sometimes rocks get buried deep inside the Earth. These buried rocks could be of any type: igneous, metamorphic, or sedimentary. The heat and pressure deep within the Earth change the rocks that are buried there. Rocks that have been changed from one form to another are called **metamorphic rocks**. Slate is a metamorphic rock.

Answer the questions.

1. If you see a rock that looks as if little pieces of rocks were glued together, what kind of rock is it?
   Ⓐ igneous rock
   Ⓑ sedimentary rock
   Ⓒ metamorphic rock

2. Igneous rock is changed to sedimentary rock when it is _____.
   Ⓐ melted
   Ⓑ exposed to high heat and pressure
   Ⓒ worn away by water and wind

3. Metamorphic rock is changed to igneous rock when it is _____.
   Ⓐ melted
   Ⓑ exposed to high heat and pressure
   Ⓒ worn away by water and wind

4. Sandstone is a _____ rock.
   Ⓐ sedimentary
   Ⓑ igneous
   Ⓒ metamorphic

5. How are igneous rocks different from metamorphic rocks? _____

_____

_____

_____

The Soil Under Your Feet

Soil is necessary for the growth of most plants in an ecosystem. All plants need nutrients to grow. Most plants get their nutrients from soil. Soil is made up of crumbled rocks and other materials. The rocks, which provide the minerals in soil, are broken up in many ways. Moving water from rain, waves, waterfalls, and rivers breaks up big pieces of rock into very small pieces. After the rock is broken up, it becomes combined with other ingredients of soil.

Once-living bits of plant and animal matter are called **humus**. Humus is an important part of soil. In soil, you can find a great variety of tiny organisms that help break down dead organisms. Some of these organisms, such as bacteria, are so small that you can see them only with a powerful microscope. Others are much like plants, but they are not green and cannot make their own food. These organisms are called fungi. The best soils for growing plants contain a lot of humus.

Write *T* if the statement is true. Write *F* if the statement is false.

_____ **1.** Soil is made completely of decayed plant material.

_____ **2.** Water has many ways of wearing down rocks.

_____ **3.** Tiny pieces of rock can be chipped away by wind.

_____ **4.** Humus consists of tiny organisms that break down living material.

_____ **5.** Fungi are organisms that look like plants but are not green and cannot make their own food.

Answer the question.

6. Describe the parts of soil and tell how soil forms.

_____

_____

_____

_____

_____

Layers of Soil

Soils differ from place to place. Soils of deciduous forests and coniferous forests are similar. They both contain a lot of humus. Soil with a lot of humus provides nutrients, which are materials that plants need to live and grow.

Soils are divided into several different layers. The uppermost layer of soil is called **topsoil**. This layer contains most of the humus that is found in the soil. The middle layer of soil is called **subsoil**. The subsoil contains less humus than topsoil. Most of the water that seeps down from above is stored in this layer. The next layer of soil is made up of large particles of rock. This is called the **parent material**. The lowest layer is called **bedrock**. Much of the mineral content of soil comes from the bedrock layer.

Soils in tropical rain forests are usually very poor in nutrients. Because of the warm, wet environment, nutrients are recycled very rapidly. Soils in the tropical rain forest are not good for raising crops.

Write _T_ if the statement is true. Write _F_ if the statement is false.

_____ **1.** All soils have the same basic parts.

_____ **2.** Rocks in the parent materials layer continue to become larger and larger.

_____ **3.** Soils of the tropical rain forest are rich in nutrients.

_____ **4.** Frequent rains in the rain forest can wash the nutrients out of the soil.

Darken the letter of the answer that best completes each sentence.

5. Leaves that fall to the ground and decay add _____ to the soil.
   Ⓐ nutrients
   Ⓑ rock particles
   Ⓒ bacteria
   Ⓓ fungi

6. Plants get most of the nutrients they need from the _____.
   Ⓐ subsoil
   Ⓑ topsoil
   Ⓒ parent material
   Ⓓ bedrock

Farming the Soil

The plant and animal life that exists on the Earth depends on soil. Soil is formed from parent material, or rock that is on or near the Earth's surface. Wind and water break down the parent material into small pieces in a process called **weathering**. Plants begin to grow in the rock pieces. Insects move in. As the plants and animals die, they break down in the soil and make it richer.

Soil can wear away faster than it forms. Soil that took thousands of years to form can be carried away in an afternoon by wind or water. There are many ways to prevent soil from wearing away, or **eroding**. Plants that cover soil can keep the wind from blowing the soil away. Farmers can plant their crops across hills rather than up and down them to help keep the soil in place. This is called contour farming.

Answer these questions.

1. Describe how soil is formed.

   _____

   _____

   _____

   _____

2. Why do farmers plant cover crops?

   _____

   _____

   _____

3. What are two different things that farmers can do to keep their soil from wearing away?

   _____

   _____

   _____

   _____

Continental Drift

Around 1912, Alfred Wegener, a geology student, hypothesized that all the continents were once joined into one supercontinent. He called this great land mass *Pangea*, which means "all Earth." He further believed that the continents had slowly moved to their current positions. He called this movement **continental drift**, and he offered much evidence to support his hypothesis. One piece of evidence was a fossil called Mesosaurus. This fossil has been found in both South America and Africa. Fossils of similar plants have also been found on different continents.

A new theory of **plate tectonics** has been built on Wegener's evidence. According to this theory, Earth's outer shell—including the crust and upper mantle—is made up of several rigid plates that float and move on the semisolid lower mantle. Much of Earth's geologic activity occurs at the boundaries of these plates.

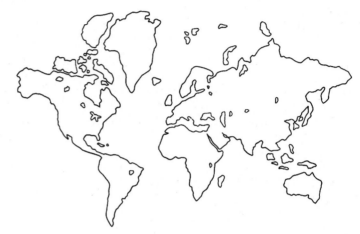

Answer these questions.

1. What does the Greek word *Pangea* mean?

_____

2. What evidence did Wegener offer for his theory of continental drift?

_____

_____

_____

3. How do the plates move?

_____

_____

4. Explain the theory of plate tectonics in terms of Earth's surface being like a jigsaw puzzle.

_____

_____

_____

_____

Do the Continents Fit Together?

Alfred Wegener believed that all the continents fit together long ago. He thought there was only one great land mass, called Pangea. Then, the continents drifted apart. Could his theory be correct? Here's an activity to see if Wegener might have been right.

You will need

- ☆ world map
- ☆ scissors
- ☆ construction paper
- ☆ glue

1. Cut out all the continents on the world map below. Be careful using the scissors.

2. Fit all the continents together like the pieces of a puzzle. Do they fit together?

3. Glue the pieces onto the sheet of construction paper. Be sure you glue them so they fit together as well as possible.

On another sheet of paper, write a paragraph describing what you think Pangea was like. Then, display your supercontinent and paragraph together.

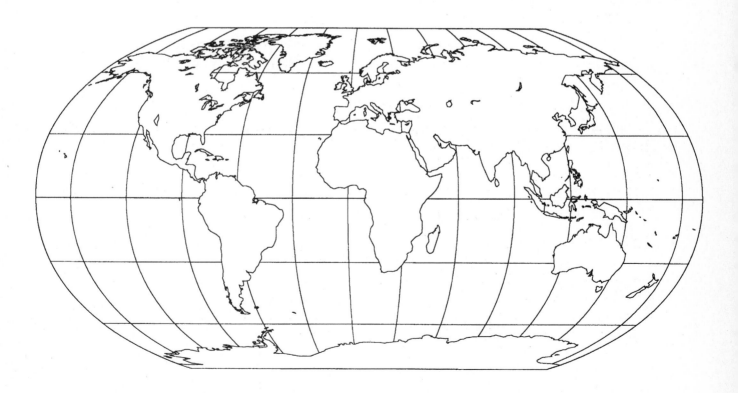

Boundaries

The Earth's crust is constantly changing. Forces within the Earth cause the crust to move. The crust is made up of about 12 sections, or **plates**. As the plates crash together, tear apart, or scrape past each other, the Earth's crust is shaken and reshaped by earthquakes, volcanoes, trenches, and mountains. Where oceanic plates collide, a **trench** is formed, and volcanoes rise up as one plate is forced under the other. Where continental plates meet, mountains form as the plates' edges are pushed up. Where an oceanic plate and a continental plate meet, a trench and a **ridge** of volcanoes line the coast. Earthquakes result wherever plates grind past each other. In fact, so many trenches, volcanoes, mountains, and earthquakes occur along the boundaries of the Pacific plate that the area is known as the Ring of Fire.

Darken the letter of the best answer.

1. When two ocean plates collide, _____.
   - Ⓐ a mountain forms
   - Ⓑ a trench forms
   - Ⓒ a coastline forms

2. When oceanic and continental plates collide, _____.
   - Ⓐ a volcano forms on the continent, and a trench forms in the ocean
   - Ⓑ a volcano forms in the ocean, and a fault forms on the continent
   - Ⓒ a rocky coastline forms between the plates

3. When two continental plates collide, _____.
   - Ⓐ large mountain ranges form
   - Ⓑ volcanoes occur
   - Ⓒ earthquakes occur

4. _____ occur when plates grind past each other.
   - Ⓐ Trenches
   - Ⓑ Volcanoes
   - Ⓒ Earthquakes

5. Which event does not occur along the Ring of Fire?
   - Ⓐ The western edge of the Pacific plate is forced under the Eurasian plate.
   - Ⓑ At the Pacific rift, new crust is forming.
   - Ⓒ The North American plate forms at the mid-Atlantic Ridge.

6. Which geologically active area is not on the Ring of Fire?
   - Ⓐ Alaska
   - Ⓑ Japan
   - Ⓒ Iceland

The Plates Move

Scientists believe that the Earth's crust is broken into 10 or 12 pieces, called plates. These plates float on the semisolid mantle. When the plates move, the continents move, too. Scientists think that the plates can move in three ways. They can collide, spread, or slip. These movements occur at the boundary lines between the plates. These boundary lines are called **faults**.

When two plates push against each other, they collide. The thin part of one plate slowly pushes its way under the thick part of another plate. The upper plate then rises. This is how some mountains are formed. Earthquakes are also common where plates collide.

Two plates can move apart, or spread. This spreading causes magma (molten rock) to squeeze up between the plates. The magma then cools and hardens into new crust. Volcanoes and earthquakes are very common where plates move apart.

Two plates can also slide past each other, or slip, causing a great grinding. The San Andreas Fault in California divides two plates. One is called the North American Plate, and the other is the Pacific Plate. These two plates slide against each other often, so earthquakes are common in California.

Answer these questions.

1. Draw arrows on the diagrams below to show the three ways that plates can move. Under each picture, write an example of what might happen when the plates move.

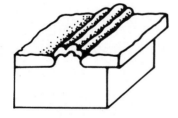 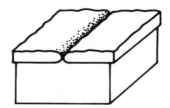 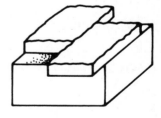

_____   _____   _____

2. Describe the three ways that plates can move.

_____

_____

_____

_____

Faults

Faults are breaks in the Earth's crust. The rock walls on either side of a fault can slip past each other when forces in the Earth move them. This movement is a major cause of earthquakes.

The three major kinds of faults are lateral faults, normal faults, and reverse faults. The difference between these faults is the way in which the rock walls move past each other.

Lateral Fault

Pressures under Earth's surface sometimes push pieces of the crust that are next to each other in opposite directions. When this happens, rock walls slip sideways past each other. This is a lateral fault. California's San Andreas is a lateral fault. It extends 1,167 km (725 mi) through the state.

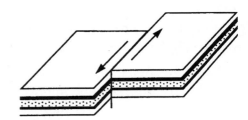

Normal Fault

Forces within the Earth can push some rock up and pull other rock down on Earth's surface. Eventually, the rock breaks, forming a normal fault. Rock walls pull away from each other along a normal fault line. One of the walls slides downward past the other. Mountain ranges can form along normal fault lines.

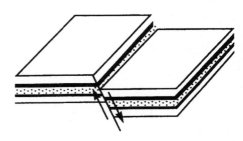

Reverse Fault

In addition to pulling rock apart, forces in the Earth can push rock together. This also causes the rock to break apart. This action forms a reverse fault. Rock walls push toward each other along a reverse fault line. One wall slides upward against the other. Mountain ranges can form along reverse fault lines, too.

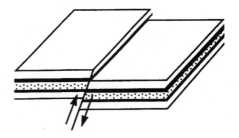

GO ON TO THE NEXT PAGE ☞

Faults, p. 2

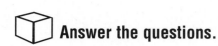 **Answer the questions.**

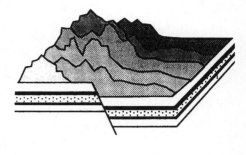

1. Explain how mountains like these might form along a fault line. What type of fault would help shape these mountains?

   _____

   _____

   _____

2. What is the difference between a normal fault and a reverse fault?

   _____

   _____

   _____

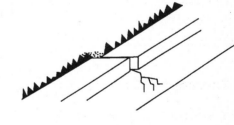

3. Explain how a fault could have caused this curb to break. What type of fault would cause it?

   _____

   _____

   _____

4. Would it be a good idea to build a building or a road on or near a fault line? Explain your answer.

   _____

   _____

   _____

Volcano!

A **volcano** is an opening in the Earth's crust through which lava escapes. A volcano forms in several steps. First, **magma** rises from the mantle and forms a pool deep in the crust. Then, cracks form in the crust above the magma pool. The magma slowly moves toward the surface through the cracks. Finally, as the magma gets nearer the surface, pressure builds up. The rocks begin to push with great force. Sometimes, the magma just oozes out. When the magma oozes out onto the surface, it is called **lava**.

Sometimes, the volcano explodes. Rock, dust, and ash are thrown into the air. Magma reaches the surface and flows out onto the land, forming a lava flow. The lava may build up and cool, creating a volcanic mountain.

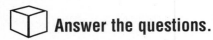 **Answer the questions.**

1. Label the magma and lava in the picture of the volcano.

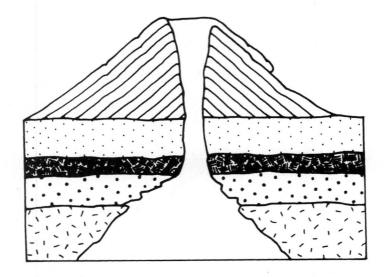

2. Below are the steps in the formation of a volcano. Number them in the correct order.

_____ The magma reaches the surface.

_____ Magma rises from the mantle.

_____ The rocks push with great force.

_____ Cracks form in the crust above the magma pool.

_____ The magma gets near the surface, and pressure builds up.

_____ The lava flows onto the surface.

_____ The magma forms a pool deep in the crust.

Geothermal Energy

The search is on for new energy sources. People are realizing that the world's supply of coal, oil, and natural gas will not last forever. Someday, these natural resources will be used up. Then, where will the Earth get its power? The Sun, nuclear power plants, windmills, and even tides, will probably provide much of the needed energy. In addition, **geothermal energy** may help.

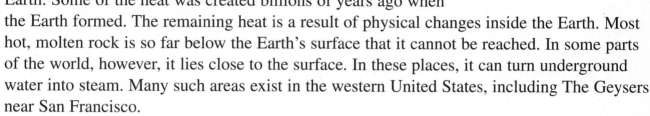

The word *geo-thermal* means "earth-heat." Geothermal energy is heat energy given off by hot, molten rock deep inside the Earth. Some of the heat was created billions of years ago when the Earth formed. The remaining heat is a result of physical changes inside the Earth. Most hot, molten rock is so far below the Earth's surface that it cannot be reached. In some parts of the world, however, it lies close to the surface. In these places, it can turn underground water into steam. Many such areas exist in the western United States, including The Geysers near San Francisco.

A power plant built at The Geysers changes geothermal energy into electricity. The steam collects in deep wells. Then, it travels through pipes to the power plant at the surface. The heat energy from the steam is used to drive turbines and generators. The steam then cools and condenses into liquid water. This water is piped into another set of wells and returned underground.

In some places, geothermal heat is released close to the surface, but no ground water is available. To harness the energy, an underground water supply must be created. One possible method would be to drill two wells deep into the rocks. Explosions could then be set off to crack the rocks between the wells. Water pumped down one well would be heated by the hot rocks and forced through the cracks to the other well. The water would become so hot that it would return to the surface as steam. The steam could be used to generate electricity.

At present, geothermal energy is used in only a few parts of the world. Perhaps in the years ahead, as other energy supplies become scarce, more people will turn to geothermal energy for their energy needs.

The sentences below tell about geothermal energy. Number them in the correct order.

_____ Steam collects in wells.

_____ The water is piped underground.

_____ The turbines are driven by steam, and electricity is produced.

_____ Steam travels through pipes to the power plant.

_____ Steam condenses into liquid water.

Earth's History

The history of the Earth is recorded in its rock layers. The age of the rocks, as well as their placement in relationship to one another, tells a story. The story is a history of the Earth. Rock layers are laid down one on top of another. The newer the rock layer, the closer it is to the surface, unless something happens to move, bend, or fold the layer. The age of rock can also be determined by the fossils in the layers.

A **fossil** is the preserved trace or remains of a once-living thing. A flat fossil of an organism or the trace of an organism that was originally made in soft soil or mud is called an **imprint**. A **mold** is a type of fossil that formed when an animal died and was covered with mud that hardened. The organism dissolved, leaving the space inside. A **cast** is a type of fossil similar to a mold. The difference is that this type of fossil is filled in with minerals.

Fossils also formed when mineral-containing water seeped into wood. The tree eventually petrified, or turned to stone. Other types of fossils were formed when organisms were preserved in sap, ice, or tar.

Answer these questions.

1. In what order are rock layers usually found?

_____

_____

2. Compare rock layers to a landfill. How are they the same? How are they different?

_____

_____

3. How do the fossils in rock layers help scientists identify the age of the rocks?

_____

_____

4. High on a mountain, you find a fossil of a clam. How could the fossil have gotten there?

_____

_____

Shaping the Earth

The shape of the land changes as you travel from place to place. On the eastern coast of the United States, you find flat low-lying land that is at **sea level**. As you move toward the west coast, you encounter different types of **landforms**, including mountains, valleys, plains, and plateaus.

The different shapes of the land are formed when rock is broken down into smaller pieces or washed away. When rock is broken down into small pieces, or sediments, the process is called **weathering**. This occurs in two ways. Rocks can be broken down by water, ice, or plants. This type of breaking down is called physical weathering. Rocks can also be broken down when substances dissolve them. This process, which often occurs in caves, is called chemical weathering.

Darken the letter of the best answer.

1. The low areas between mountains are called _____.
   - Ⓐ plateaus
   - Ⓑ valleys
   - Ⓒ plains

2. Crops grow best _____.
   - Ⓐ on mountains
   - Ⓑ in valleys
   - Ⓒ on plains

3. What type of map shows the rock layers inside a landform?
   - Ⓐ a road map
   - Ⓑ an elevation map
   - Ⓒ a cross-section map

4. The average level of the sea where it meets the land is called _____.
   - Ⓐ sea level
   - Ⓑ the shore
   - Ⓒ ground zero

5. Water can break up rocks when it freezes because _____.
   - Ⓐ ice is hard
   - Ⓑ water expands when it freezes
   - Ⓒ rocks don't like the cold

6. At the foot of a cliff is a rock beach. The beach is the same color as the rocks in the cliff because rocks have broken off the cliff to form the beach. This is an example of _____.
   - Ⓐ physical weathering
   - Ⓑ chemical weathering
   - Ⓒ erosion

7. Stone columns form inside a cave. This is an example of _____.
   - Ⓐ physical weathering
   - Ⓑ chemical weathering
   - Ⓒ erosion

Erosion

Rocks are changed when weathered rock and soil move from one place to another. This process is called **erosion**. Erosion is most often caused by moving water, but it can also be caused by gravity, by wind, and by huge moving sheets of ice, or **glaciers**.

Moving water is most often found in the form of rivers. As the rivers carry their bits of rock and soil toward the ocean, the land changes shape. As the river water gets close to the ocean, it slows down. When this happens, some of the rock and soil fall out of the water. These bits of rock, sand, and soil collect at the mouth of the river and form a **delta**. This land is rich in nutrients and is very good for growing crops.

Answer these questions.

1. Explain how gravity causes erosion.

_____

_____

2. How is weathering different from erosion?

_____

_____

_____

3. How do glaciers cause erosion?

_____

_____

_____

4. Compare erosion caused by rivers and erosion caused by glaciers.

_____

_____

_____

Interpreting Map Data

Data is information given to you or information that you gather during activities. When you interpret data, you decide what it means. When you read a map, you are interpreting data. The map below shows the area surrounding Big Sister Mesa. A mesa is a small, high plateau.

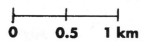 Study the map. Then, answer the questions.

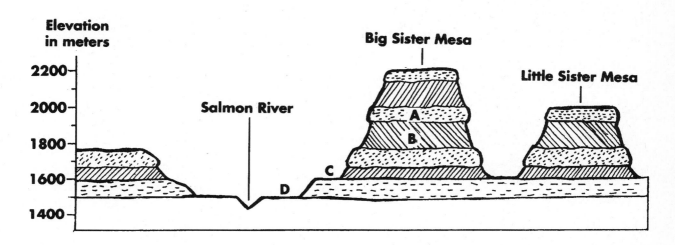

1. *Mesa* means "table" in Spanish. By looking at the cross-section map, can you tell how this landform got its name? Explain.

   _____

2. What is the elevation of Big Sister Mesa? the elevation of Little Sister Mesa? the elevation of the Salmon River?

   _____

3. Which rock is softer: the rock in layer A or in layer B? Explain your answer.

   _____

   _____

4. During the spring, the Salmon River sometimes rises more than 7 meters above its banks. Would a home built at point C be in danger from the flood? What about a home at point D? How can you tell?

   _____

   _____

   _____

The Compass

Scientists think that the Earth's interior acts something like a bar magnet. This gives the Earth north and south magnetic poles. A magnetic field originates at the poles and surrounds the Earth. This magnetic field has been detected by astronauts in space. They floated magnets in their space capsules and found these magnets moved to stay in line with the Earth's magnetic field. On the Earth, a **compass** with a magnetized needle also lines up with the Earth's magnetic field. You can make a compass in this activity.

You will need

☆ 1 styrofoam cup or a piece of cork   ☆ scissors

☆ 1 small bowl or flat dish of water   ☆ a bar magnet

☆ a sewing needle

1. Cut a small piece of styrofoam about 1 in. (2.5 cm) square.
   CAUTION: Be careful when handling the scissors.

2. Use one end of the bar magnet to stroke the needle. Do not rub back and forth, but stroke from the middle of the needle toward the point, 10 times.

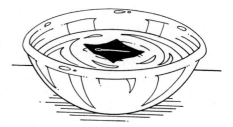

3. Set the needle on the styrofoam or cork and float it in the middle of the dish of water.

4. Be sure the area is clear of any large metal objects that could attract the needle. The table should not contain any metal parts.

5. The point of the needle should point north. If you have a commercial compass, use it to test the accuracy of yours.

Answer these questions.

1. Does your compass point north? How do you know?

   _____

   _____

2. Would this compass work on the Moon? Why or why not?

   _____

   _____

Evaporation and Temperature

Water vapor in the air affects the way we feel. The amount of water vapor in the air is called **humidity**. On a hot summer day when the humidity is high, the air feels sticky. On hot, humid days, the liquid you perspire is not easily evaporated. The air just cannot hold much more moisture. This is part of the reason you feel hot and sticky. What effect does evaporation have on your body? You can find out with this activity.

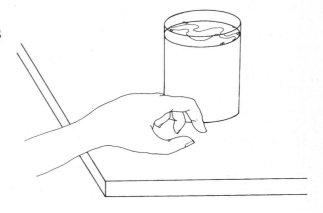

1. Moisten the back of your hand with some water. Wait a few seconds, then blow across the wet spot. How does the wet spot feel?

   _____

2. Moisten the back of the same hand again. Blow across the wet spot. Blow across the back of your other hand, too.

 Answer these questions.

1. How does your wet hand feel compared with your dry hand when you blow across them?

   _____

   _____

2. What happens to the moisture when you blow across it?

   _____

3. What difference do you feel in the temperature of your hand when you blow across the wet spot?

   _____

   _____

4. Does evaporation make the temperature of a surface warmer or cooler?

   _____

   _____

   _____

Relative Humidity

Humidity is the amount of water vapor in the air. **Relative humidity** is the amount of water vapor in the air compared to the amount of water vapor the air can hold. Meteorologists use a psychrometer to measure relative humidity. Here's how to make a simple psychrometer.

You will need

- ★ 2 Celsius thermometers
- ★ 2 pieces of stiff cardboard (23 x 30 cm)
- ★ transparent tape
- ★ 2 or 3 books
- ★ 8-cm piece of woven shoelace (forms a tube)
- ★ small cup of water
- ★ clock

1. Tape the two thermometers to one piece of cardboard, as shown in the diagram.

2. Lay this piece of cardboard on the books.

3. Slip the shoelace tube over the bulb of one thermometer. Let the other end of the tube hang into the cup of water under the bulb. This is the wet-bulb thermometer. The other is the dry-bulb thermometer.

4. Fan the bulbs with the other piece of cardboard. Wait until the wet-bulb temperature stays the same for a minute. Record the wet-bulb and dry-bulb temperatures.

5. Subtract the smaller number from the larger one to find the difference between the two temperatures.

GO ON TO THE NEXT PAGE ☞

Name _____   Date _____

Relative Humidity, p. 2

6. Use the chart below to find relative humidity. First, on the left-hand side of the chart, find the row for the dry-bulb temperature. Then, at the top of the chart, find the column for the difference between the two temperatures. The number where the row and column meet is the relative humidity.

RELATIVE HUMIDITY (%)

Dry-bulb (°C)	Difference between wet-bulb and dry-bulb temperatures (°C)																	
	1°	2°	3°	4°	5°	6°	7°	8°	9°	10°	11°	12°	13°	14°	15°	16°	17°	18°
11°	89	78	67	56	46	36	27	18	9									
12°	89	78	68	58	48	39	29	21	12									
13°	89	79	69	59	50	41	32	23	15	7								
14°	90	79	70	60	51	42	34	26	18	10								
15°	90	80	71	61	53	44	36	27	20	13	6							
16°	90	81	71	63	54	46	38	30	23	15	8							
17°	90	81	72	64	55	47	40	32	25	18	11							
18°	91	82	73	65	57	49	41	34	27	20	14	7						
19°	91	82	74	65	58	50	43	36	29	22	16	10						
20°	91	83	74	66	59	51	44	37	31	24	18	12	6					
21°	91	83	75	67	60	53	46	39	32	26	20	14	9					
22°	92	83	76	68	61	54	47	40	34	28	22	17	11	6				
23°	92	84	76	69	62	55	48	42	36	30	24	19	13	8				
24°	92	84	77	69	62	56	49	43	37	31	26	20	15	10	5			
25°	92	84	77	70	63	57	50	44	39	33	28	22	17	12	8			
26°	92	85	78	71	64	58	51	46	40	34	29	24	19	14	10	5		
27°	92	85	78	71	65	58	52	47	41	36	31	26	21	16	12	7		
28°	93	85	78	72	65	59	53	48	42	37	32	27	22	18	13	9	5	
29°	93	86	79	72	66	60	54	49	43	38	33	28	24	19	15	11	7	
30°	93	86	79	73	67	61	55	50	44	39	35	30	25	21	17	13	9	5

Answer these questions.

1. What relative humidity reading did you get?

   _____

2. Predict how your classroom's relative humidity compares with the relative humidity outside. Test your prediction. How accurate was it?

   _____

   _____

3. Predict how your readings would be different outside on a rainy day. Test your prediction. How accurate was it?

   _____

   _____

   _____

   _____

What Are the Oceans?

The vast majority of the Earth's water is in its **oceans**. Along with rivers and lakes, oceans provide important routes of transportation. Oceans cover more than two thirds of Earth's surface. Oceans are wide and deep bodies of water. Although there are living things at all depths of the oceans, much of the life is found in the top 200 meters of water.

The ocean floor is not a flat, featureless surface. Because of Earth's processes, there are mountains, hills, slopes, plains, and valleys at different depths in the oceans. The ocean floor shows as much difference below the water as the continents show above it.

Oceans are full of salt water, not fresh water. Salt water has some properties that make it different from fresh water. One property is that objects float more easily in salt water than in fresh water. Another property is that salt water freezes more slowly than fresh water.

▣ Darken the letter of the answer that best completes each sentence.

1. Oceans cover more than _____ of the Earth's surface.
   Ⓐ one fourth
   Ⓑ one third
   Ⓒ one half
   Ⓓ two thirds

2. Compared to fresh water, salt water _____.
   Ⓐ freezes in about the same time
   Ⓑ freezes much more rapidly
   Ⓒ freezes more slowly
   Ⓓ doesn't ever freeze

▣ Answer this question.

3. Describe two ways in which salt water is different from fresh water.

_____

_____

_____

_____

_____

Name _____ Date _____

Graphing the World's Oceans

Three of the world's major oceans are the Atlantic, Pacific, and Indian. In this activity you will compare these oceans.

You will need

★ a ruler ★ colored pencils

Use the data given in the chart to make two bar graphs. On one graph show the depths of the three oceans. On the other graph show the area covered by each.

Ocean	Depth in Meters	Area in Millions of Square Kilometers
Atlantic	3,925	82 sq km
Indian	3,963	73 sq km
Pacific	4,282	165 sq km

DEPTHS OF THE OCEANS

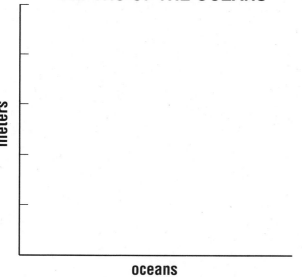

meters

oceans

AREAS OF THE OCEANS

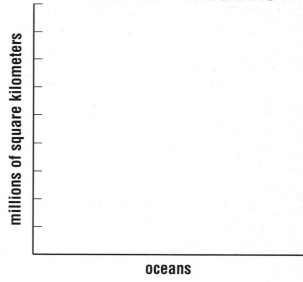

millions of square kilometers

oceans

Answer these questions.

1. Which ocean is the deepest? _____

2. Which ocean covers the smallest area? _____

3. Which ocean is shallowest? _____

The Ocean Floor

Look at the diagram of the ocean floor. Then, read the descriptions of different areas of the ocean floor. Write the numeral of each description in the correct box on the diagram.

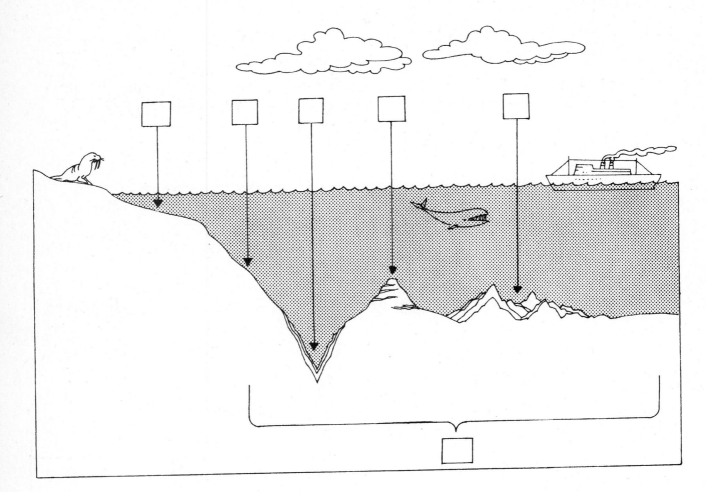

1. The continental shelf is the flat floor that slopes down from the coasts of the continents. The waters here are not deep and contain many kinds of plants and animals.
2. Trenches are narrow deep valleys in the ocean floor.
3. Mid-ocean ridges are long chains of mountains that run along the floor of the oceans.
4. The ocean basin is the very deep part of the ocean floor. Sunlight cannot reach the bottom of the ocean basin.
5. The continental slope begins as the ocean floor falls steeply away from the continental shelf.
6. Underwater volcanic mountains dot the floor of the ocean basin.

Waves and Currents

Water in the ocean moves in a number of ways. **Waves** are movements of ocean water that can be caused by earthquakes or underwater landslides. Most commonly, waves are caused by the wind. The more the water is disturbed, the higher the waves are.

Currents are strong flows of water, much like great rivers flowing over the surface of the oceans. Winds can also cause currents. Currents flow in the direction that winds blow most of the time.

Answer these questions.

1. Most ocean waves are caused by _____.
   Ⓐ winds   Ⓑ underwater landslides   Ⓒ earthquakes   Ⓓ ships

2. Steady, slow winds that follow the same paths most of the time can cause _____.
   Ⓐ earthquake waves   Ⓑ sonar   Ⓒ surface currents   Ⓓ trenches

3. Use the chart below to name two ways in which waves and currents are similar and two ways in which they are different.

CHARACTERISTICS OF WAVES AND CURRENTS

Waves	Currents
• Occur in water.	• Occur in water.
• Occur in oceans.	• Occur in oceans.
• Can be caused by wind, earthquakes, and underwater landslides.	• Can be caused by wind.
• Waves are swells.	• Currents are long rivers of water in the ocean.

_____

_____

_____

_____

Observing Currents in an Ocean Model

Ocean currents can be caused by differences in ocean temperatures. In this activity you will find out why temperature differences lead to these changes.

You will need

- ☆ aquarium with water
- ☆ 2 thermometers
- ☆ tape
- ☆ watch
- ☆ ice cube tinted with food coloring

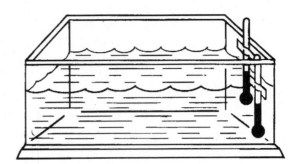

1. Set up the aquarium and thermometers as shown in the drawing. Tape one thermometer to the inside of the aquarium so that it will measure the water temperature at the top of the aquarium. Tape the other thermometer so that it measures the water temperature at the bottom of the aquarium.

2. Fill the aquarium and read the temperature of the water near each thermometer. Record the temperatures on the chart.

Temperature	Top	Bottom
At start		
1 minute		
2 minutes		
3 minutes		
4 minutes		

3. Place the ice cube near the thermometer that measures the water temperature at the top of the aquarium.

4. Read the temperature of the water near each thermometer every minute for four minutes. Record the temperatures in the chart. Observe how the cold, colored water moves as the ice cube melts.

Answer these questions on another piece of paper.

1. Which thermometer showed the greatest temperature change?

2. Why did the temperature decrease at the bottom of the aquarium when the ice cube was placed at the top?

3. How does this experiment relate to ocean currents?

Salty Currents

Density is the amount of mass in a certain volume. Suppose that two materials take up the same amount of space, but have different masses. Then, these two materials would have different densities. The material with the greater mass has the greater density. You can find out how salt affects the density of water. You can also see the effect of density on currents.

You will need

* ☆ 2 identical measuring spoons
* ☆ 2 identical clear cups
* ☆ blue food coloring
* ☆ red food coloring
* ☆ wax pencil
* ☆ measuring cup
* ☆ eyedropper
* ☆ water
* ☆ balance
* ☆ salt
* ☆ pencil

1. Use the wax pencil to label the cups **Cup 1** and **Cup 2**. Label the spoons **S1** and **S2**. Always use S1 with Cup 1 and S2 with Cup 2. This will prevent accidentally adding extra salt to either cup.

2. Add 125 mL of water to each cup. Put one cup on each side of the balance. Do they have the same mass? _____ (If the cups do not balance, adjust the volume of water until they do.) Remove the cups from the balance.

3. With S1, add 1 teaspoon of salt to Cup 1. Stir. With S2, add 4 teaspoons of salt to Cup 2. Stir.

4. Place the cups on the balance. Which cup has the greater mass? _____
   Why? _____ Which cup has the greater density? _____
   Remove the cups from the balance.

5. Add three drops of red food coloring to Cup 1. Stir with S1. Add three drops of blue coloring to Cup 2. Stir with S2.

6. Add a dropperful of blue water from Cup 2 to one edge of the water in Cup 1. What happens? _____ Why? _____

7. Which part of the oceans do you think are the saltier, the top or the bottom? _____

8. What effect does a difference in density have on ocean waters?

   _____

Waves on the Beach

Waves crash on beaches hour after hour, day after day. What effect do the constant waves have on the beach? Do waves cause erosion? This activity will help you to find out.

You will need

★ disposable aluminum roasting pan

★ sand

★ 2 wooden blocks

★ water

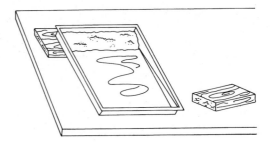

1. Fill one end of the pan with sand. Shape the sand into a sloping "beach."

2. Place one wooden block under the beach end of the pan so that the pan is sloping.

3. Gently pour water into the end of the pan opposite the beach. Stop pouring when the level of the water meets the beach.

4. Hold the other wooden block in the water at the end of the pan opposite the beach. Make waves by slowly moving the block up and down about ten times.

5. Increase the force of the waves by pushing harder and more rapidly on the block. The waves that result represent storm waves. Do this ten times, too.

 Answer these questions.

1. How was the beach changed by the gentle waves?

_____

_____

2. How did the storm waves change the beach?

_____

_____

3. Where was some of the sand moved?

_____

_____

4. What are the effects of waves on real beaches?

_____

_____

What Tide Is It?

Tides are caused by the Moon's gravitational pull on the Earth and on the bodies of water on it. The Moon causes the water on the side of the Earth nearest to it to rise up in a high tide. The water on the opposite side of the Earth also rises up in a high tide as the solid Earth under it is pulled toward the Moon. Low tides occur in between these places as water flows toward the high tides.

The Earth rotates on its axis once every 24 hours, so the Moon causes high tides at any one location twice every day. High tides would occur every 12 hours, except for one thing. The Moon revolves around the Earth at the same time as the Earth is rotating. When the Earth completes one revolution, the Moon has moved 13 degrees in the same direction. Therefore, the Earth has to rotate a little more before the Moon is over the same place that it was 24 hours earlier.

For this reason, high tides are slightly more than 12 hours apart. The afternoon high tide on one day is about 12 hours and 50 minutes later than the afternoon high tide on the previous day, and the same holds true for the low tides.

The chart below lists the tides for Cape May, New Jersey, for a period of one week. Use the chart to help you answer the questions.

TIDES FOR CAPE MAY, NEW JERSEY

	Low		High	
	A.M.	P.M.	A.M.	P.M.
Tuesday	9:16	9:28	2:43	3:30
Wednesday	10:09	10:25	3:52	4:33
Thursday	11:00	11:20	4:54	5:28
Friday	11:50	12:07	5:48	6:17
Saturday	12:14	12:39	6:37	7:04
Sunday	1:06	1:28	7:25	7:51
Monday	1:57	2:15	8:12	8:38

GO ON TO THE NEXT PAGE ☞

What Tide Is It?, p. 2

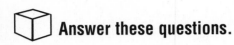 **Answer these questions.**

1. How many low tides occur each day?

_____

2. About how much time elapses between high tides on the same day?

_____

3. Complete the chart to show how much time elapsed between low tides and high tides on each day. The first day has been done for you.

Day	Time Between Low Tides	Time Between High Tides
Tuesday	12 hr 12 min	12 hr 47 min
Wednesday		
Thursday		
Friday		
Saturday		
Sunday		
Monday		

4. How much later is the A.M. high tide on Friday than the A.M. high tide on Thursday?

_____

5. How much later is the P.M. low tide on Sunday than the P.M. low tide on Saturday?

_____

Lighter Than Water?

You know that oil is lighter than water. You also know that warm air is lighter than cold air. Can one kind of water be lighter than another? Try this activity to find out.

You will need

- ☆ 3 cups
- ☆ tap water
- ☆ measuring spoons
- ☆ salt
- ☆ masking tape
- ☆ 3 colors of food coloring
- ☆ 3 drinking straws
- ☆ clear plastic glass

1. Fill each cup half full of water. In one cup, add 2 teaspoons of salt to the water. Make a masking-tape label that tells how much salt you added, and attach it to the cup. Stir until the salt is dissolved.

2. Add 4 teaspoons of salt to another cup of water. Make a masking-tape label that records how much salt you added, and attach it to the cup. Stir until the salt is dissolved. Leave one cup with no salt.

3. Add a few drops of a different food coloring to each cup. Stir the water in the cups.

4. Put a straw into the water that had 4 teaspoons of salt added. Put your finger over the opening and move the straw over the clear plastic glass. Let the water run into the clear glass. Using another straw, repeat the process for the water containing 2 teaspoons of salt. Carefully let the water run into the clear glass on top of the very salty water. Repeat the process with the plain water.

Answer these questions.

1. Label the levels in the diagram.

2. What can you tell about salty water from this diagram?

_____

_____

3. In an estuary, salt water from the ocean meets fresh water from a river. Where do you think the ocean water would be in an estuary: on the top or on the bottom?

_____

_____

Earth's Atmosphere

We live on the crust of the Earth. We have food and water. But another part of the Earth's structure is needed to keep us alive. That part is called the **atmosphere**. The atmosphere is about 500 miles (800 km) high, and it is held in place by the Earth's gravity. The atmosphere has four layers.

Closest to the Earth is the **troposphere**, the layer in which we live. The troposphere is only a thin band of the atmosphere, about 5 to 10 miles (8–16 km) thick. All the Earth's weather occurs in the troposphere. The troposphere also contains the air we need to live. The air in the troposphere is about 80 percent nitrogen and 20 percent oxygen. There are also small amounts of other gases, including argon and carbon dioxide.

Above the troposphere is the **stratosphere**, a layer that is from about 5 to 50 miles (8–80 km) high. The stratosphere is similar to the troposphere in its composition, but in the stratosphere people need extra oxygen to breathe. The stratosphere has only a few clouds. These clouds are mostly made of ice crystals. In the stratosphere are the fast-moving winds known as the jet stream. The air in the lower part of the stratosphere is cold. In the upper part of the stratosphere, the temperature increases. The important ozone layer is in the upper stratosphere. The ozone absorbs ultraviolet energy from the Sun, which causes the temperature there to rise. The ozone layer is important because it protects creatures on the Earth from the harmful ultraviolet rays.

Above the stratosphere is the **ionosphere**, which stretches from about 50 miles to about 300 miles (80–500 km) above the Earth. There is almost no air in the ionosphere. The natural displays of light called auroras occur in the ionosphere.

The top layer of the atmosphere is called the **exosphere**. It begins about 300 miles (500 km) above the Earth, but it has no real top boundary. This layer is the beginning of what we call outer space. The exosphere contains mostly oxygen and helium gases. This layer also has a very high temperature, up to several thousand degrees.

 Label the layers of the Earth's atmosphere in the picture. Write *troposphere*, *stratosphere*, *ionosphere*, or *exosphere* on the correct line.

Name _____   Date _____

The Sun and Weather

The Sun is the most important factor in producing **weather**. The Sun influences Earth's weather in two ways. First, Earth's land and water are warmed by the Sun's energy. Because land heats and cools more quickly than water, the air above land heats and cools more quickly than the air above water. Warm air is less dense than cold air, so it rises. As warm air rises, it cools and becomes more dense. Then, the cool, dense air sinks. The movement of air from places where it is dense to places where it is less dense is wind. Temperature differences between mountains and valleys and between land and sea cause local winds. There are general wind patterns also, caused by the movement of air between the equator and the poles. These patterns are the prevailing winds.

The second way in which the Sun influences Earth's weather is through the **water cycle**. As the Sun warms the Earth's surface, water evaporates from the oceans into the air. The warmer the air, the more moisture it can hold. As the warm, moist air rises it cools, and the moisture condenses, forming fog or clouds. Clouds are of three basic types: cirrus, stratus, and cumulus. When cloud droplets or ice crystals are too large to be suspended in air, they fall as precipitation.

Answer these questions.

1. In what two ways does the Sun affect the weather?

_____

2. What causes wind?

_____

_____

3. Explain why the wind blows from the ocean toward the land on a summer day, and from the land toward the ocean on a summer night.

_____

_____

_____

4. What are the three basic types of clouds?

_____

5. How do clouds form?

_____

_____

Air Masses

A large body of air with the same temperature, pressure, and humidity is called an **air mass**. Air masses are produced when air remains over one part of the Earth's surface for a long time. These great air masses move slowly across the Earth's surface. These moving air masses take on the characteristics of the surface beneath them. Air moving over a warm surface is warmed, and air moving over a cold surface is cooled. Air moving over water becomes moist, and air moving over land becomes drier. As it moves, the air mass causes changes in the weather of an area.

A **front** is a line or boundary between air masses. The passage of a front usually produces changes in temperature, pressure, wind speed and direction, and humidity. The air masses clash along the front, so weather along a front is often stormy. A **cold front** occurs when a cold air mass replaces a warm air mass. Weather along a cold front often includes thunderstorms with much precipitation. A **warm front** occurs when a warm air mass replaces a cold air mass. Precipitation may also occur along a warm front, but the precipitation is usually not as heavy as along a cold front. A **stationary front** occurs when air masses meet without moving. A stationary front may produce an extended period of precipitation.

 Answer these questions on another sheet of paper.

1. What characteristics do all air masses have in common?
2. What are the characteristics of an air mass over land?
3. What are the characteristics of an air mass over water?
4. What three kinds of fronts can form between air masses?
5. Describe the air masses that affect the weather in the summer and in the winter where you live.

Storm Warning

Certain weather conditions may lead to violent **storms** that can harm people and damage their property. As warm, moist air rises, it almost always produces storms with dark clouds, high winds, and heavy precipitation. Some storms become severe, with thunder and lightning, a huge electric spark that travels from cloud to cloud or from clouds to the ground. Lightning can be dangerous if a person or an object is in its path. In some thunderstorms, hail forms as rain freezes in the clouds and forms ice. If the precipitation is heavy enough or lasts long enough, flooding can occur.

A line of violent thunderstorms, called a **squall line**, sometimes accompanies the passage of a cold front. Warm air rises rapidly in front of the advancing cold air, producing an area of very low pressure. Air rushes into the low-pressure area from all sides, resulting in a twisting, funnel-shaped storm called a **tornado**. The extremely high winds of a tornado can destroy almost everything in its path.

Over tropical oceans in summer months, conditions sometimes cause very warm, moist air to rise rapidly, forming a large, intense storm called a **hurricane**. A fully developed hurricane has bands of clouds spinning around a calm eye. As a hurricane nears land, strong winds, large waves, high tides, and torrential rains can cause extensive damage.

When cold air from the poles meets warm air from the tropics, a large spinning storm forms. In winter, these storms sometimes combine heavy snow and strong winds to produce a **blizzard**. Deep, drifting snow and bitter-cold temperatures make blizzards very dangerous.

Darken the letter of the answer that best completes each sentence.

1. Where warm and cold air masses meet, _____.
   - Ⓐ it never rains
   - Ⓑ a squall line may form
   - Ⓒ a hurricane may form

2. A hurricane may develop in _____.
   - Ⓐ a cold polar ocean
   - Ⓑ a warm tropical ocean
   - Ⓒ any ocean

3. A blizzard may develop where _____.
   - Ⓐ a polar air mass meets a cold, moist air mass
   - Ⓑ two warm air masses meet
   - Ⓒ a polar air mass meets a warm, moist air mass

Answer these questions on another sheet of paper.

4. What are the main characteristics of a tornado?
5. On another sheet of paper, describe what you would do if you were caught in a tornado, hurricane, or blizzard.

Different Places, Different Weather

Climates are long-term weather patterns. Many factors cause climates to vary from place to place. The average weather of a particular place over a long period of time is known as climate. The climate of an area is determined by the air masses associated with its location on the Earth's surface. The climate of regions near the equator is tropical because of warm air masses. Cold air masses near the poles produce climates that are polar. The weather in tropical and polar climates remains stable throughout the year. Between the equator and the poles are regions with climates that are temperate. Temperate climates are affected by both warm and cold air masses at different times of the year, so the weather changes with the seasons.

Local weather conditions often produce **microclimates**, areas where climates are different from those of surrounding areas. Mountain shadows and heat islands are examples of microclimates. Large bodies of water and ocean currents tend to moderate climates. Altitude also affects climate. Going up a mountain is similar to traveling toward the poles; the climate generally gets colder. Human activity can also affect climate. The release of carbon dioxide from the burning of fuels produces a **greenhouse effect**, an increase in temperature. A prolonged greenhouse effect could lead to global warming, a permanent change in Earth's climates.

Write the name of the climate after each description.

1. This climatic zone is located near the equator. In this zone, the average temperature in the coldest months is 18 degrees C. This is higher than the average temperature of the

   warmest months in the polar zone. _____

2. The two regions of this climatic zone are located near the poles. In this zone, the warmest months average less than 10 degrees C. This is lower than the average

   temperature of the coldest months in the tropical zone._____

3. The two regions of this climatic zone are located between the climatic zone near the equator and the climatic zone located near each pole. The average temperature of the coldest months is lower than that of the tropical zone, while the average temperature of

   the warmest months is higher than that of the polar zone. _____

Answer these questions on another sheet of paper.

4. How is today's weather related to the climate where you live?
5. Draw an example of a microclimate.

The Solar System

Earth is the third planet from the Sun. The **solar system** can be divided into the inner planets and the outer planets. The inner planets include Mercury, Venus, Earth, and Mars. The outer planets include Jupiter, Saturn, Uranus, Neptune, and Pluto. Because distances in the solar system are so great, astronomers use a measurement called an AU, or astronomical unit, which is the distance between the Earth and the Sun.

Mercury is the planet closest to the Sun. It is about the size of Earth's moon. Mercury's surface is rocky, and the planet has little or no atmosphere. Venus, the second planet from the sun, is about the size of Earth. Venus has a rocky surface and a hot, thick atmosphere. Earth, the third planet from the Sun, has a rocky surface and is mostly covered with water. Earth's atmosphere keeps the temperature moderate and supports life. Earth is the first planet from the Sun to have a moon, or satellite. Mars, the fourth planet from the Sun, is about half the size of Earth. Mars has a rocky surface, a thin atmosphere, and two moons. Between the inner planets and the outer planets is a belt of asteroids, containing thousands of large pieces of rock, which may be part of an unformed planet.

Jupiter, the fifth planet from the Sun, is larger than all the other planets combined. Most of Jupiter is a thick, swirling mass of clouds. Jupiter has at least 17 moons and a small, thin ring. Saturn, the sixth planet from the Sun, is similar to Jupiter but much smaller. Saturn has a much larger ring system than Jupiter. Uranus and Neptune, the seventh and eighth planets, are also similar to Jupiter and Saturn. Pluto, the last planet from the Sun, is very different from the other outer planets. It is rocky and very small. Pluto has one moon, Charon.

 Label the Sun, the planets, and the asteroid belt in this diagram of the solar system.

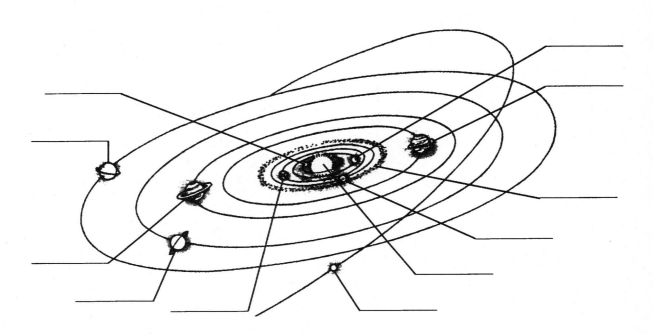

Name _____ Date _____

Make a Scale Model of the Planets

To see how far the planets are from the Sun and each other, make a scale model.

You will need

★ strip of adding machine tape 6 m (20 ft) long   ★ metric ruler

1. Draw a tiny circle near one end of the tape. Label it *Sun*.

2. Look at the distances in the drawing. Mercury is 58 million km from the Sun. Let 1 mm equal 1 million km. Measure 58 mm from the dot you labeled the Sun and make another dot. Label it *Mercury*.

3. For each planet let 1 mm equal 1 million km. Measure the distances on your tape, and make a dot for each planet. Label each planet.

 Answer these questions.

1. Look at the spacing between the inner planets. Look at the spacing between the outer planets. What difference do you see?

_____

_____

2. Your scale drawing does not include asteroids. Where would you add them to your drawing?

_____

_____

3. If you were to add a comet to your scale model, where would its orbit be placed?

_____

_____

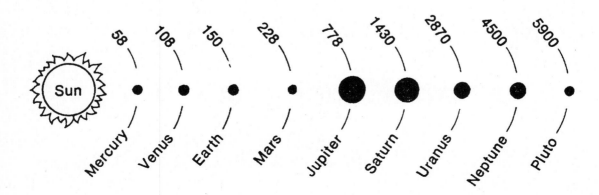

The Earth Moves

The Earth moves constantly, **rotating** on its axis, which causes the day and night cycle. The Earth also **revolves** around the Sun and **tilts** on its axis. As the tilt changes, parts of the Earth are closer to the Sun. The **seasons** occur as a result of the Earth's tilt on its axis. During the six months that the North Pole is tilted toward the Sun, the Northern Hemisphere gets more sunlight than the Southern Hemisphere does. The atmosphere is warmer then in the Northern Hemisphere, resulting in warmer weather. During the time the North Pole is tilted toward the Sun, the Northern Hemisphere experiences late spring, summer, and early fall. At the same time, the Southern Hemisphere is having late fall, winter, and early spring. The Northern Hemisphere experiences these later seasons when the North Pole is tilted away from the Sun.

The summer and winter **solstices** occur in late June and December each year. The summer solstice is the day your hemisphere of the Earth is tilted most toward the Sun. This day has the greatest number of hours of daylight. The winter solstice is the day your hemisphere is tilted most away from the Sun. This day has the fewest hours of daylight.

The spring (vernal) and fall (autumnal) **equinoxes** occur in late March and September each year. At the time of these two equinoxes, the Sun is directly above the equator, and each hemisphere of the Earth receives equal numbers of hours of sunlight and darkness.

On the diagram below, identify and label the *summer solstice, winter solstice, spring equinox,* and *fall equinox*.

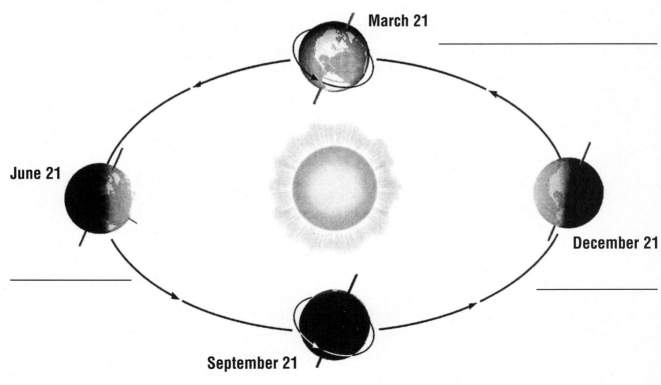

Calendar Counting

A **calendar** is a device that people use to measure time. Most calendars show about one solar year, the time it takes Earth to make one complete revolution around the Sun. A calendar year consists of 365 days. However, a solar year is actually 365 days, 5 hours, 48 minutes, and 46 seconds long! For this reason, we have leap years. A leap year consists of 366 days and occurs once every four years. The extra day in the leap year makes up for the time beyond 365 days in every solar year.

Some ancient peoples used a calendar based on the phases of the Moon. This kind of calendar is called a lunar calendar and is made up of 12 lunar months. A lunar month is the amount of time it takes the Moon to pass through all of its phases, or $29\frac{1}{2}$ days. Problems arose with this calendar because it did not match the revolution of Earth around the Sun. For this reason, the lunar calendar was discarded in favor of the solar calendar.

1	2	3	4	5	6	7
8	9	10	11	12	13	14
15	16	17	18	19	20	21
22	23	24	25	26	27	28
29	30	31				

Solar Calendar
12 Months

1	2	3	4	5	6	7
8	9	10	11	12	13	14
15	16	17	18	19	20	21
22	23	24	25	26	27	28
29	$29\frac{1}{2}$					

Lunar Calendar
12⅓ Months

Answer these questions.

1. If a lunar month consists of $29\frac{1}{2}$ days, how long is one lunar year?

_____

2. What is the difference, in days, between a lunar year and a solar year?

_____

3. Ted is exactly 28 years old. He wants to determine his age in lunar years. Write the steps Ted should follow to determine his lunar age. What is Ted's lunar age in years?

_____

Observing an Earth/Moon Model

The Moon revolves around the Earth. You can make a model to show this action.

You will need

⭐ a table-tennis ball ⭐ a tennis ball

⭐ 2 pieces of string ⭐ a plastic drinking straw

1. Tie one string tightly around the tennis ball. Pass one end of the string through the plastic straw. Then, tie the other end tightly around the table-tennis ball as shown below.

2. Find the balance point of the straw. Then, hang the straw and balls from the other string.

3. Wind up the system by turning the table-tennis ball around the string. Turn the ball around about 20 times.

4. Allow the string to unwind. As it does, watch the motion of the two balls.

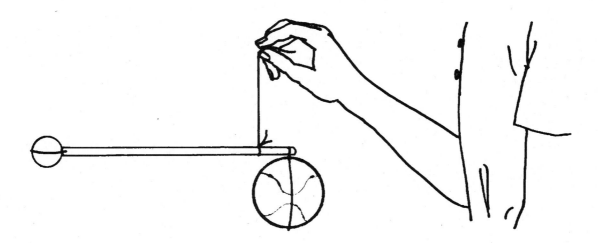

🧊 Answer these questions.

1. Where is the place around which the tennis ball (Earth) revolved?

_____

2. Where is the place around which the table-tennis ball (Moon) revolved?

_____

3. Did the tennis and table-tennis balls revolve around the same point?

_____

The Stars Above

To someone on Earth, the **stars** look as if they are attached to the inside of a huge ball. Astronomers call this ball the **celestial sphere**. Since the Earth rotates on its axis from west to east, the celestial sphere seems to rotate from east to west, so most stars seem to rise in the east and set in the west, like the Sun. However, some stars, called **circumpolar stars**, are always above the horizon.

Throughout the year, different star patterns, or **constellations**, appear on the celestial sphere. Ancient astronomers noted that the Sun seemed to move through the same constellations year after year. They named this path the ecliptic. The 12 constellations that lie on the path of the ecliptic are called the **zodiac**.

Earth's nearest star, the Sun, is about 1.4 billion kilometers in diameter. Like all stars, the Sun is a glowing globe of hot gas. The hydrogen at the Sun's core is compressed and heated by the weight of its outer layers to a temperature of 14 million degrees C. Its corona, or atmosphere, is a cool 2 million degrees C. The Sun, like all the other stars in the universe, is a source of tremendous energy.

Darken the letter of the answer that best completes each sentence.

1. The 12 constellations that lie on the path of the ecliptic are also known as the _____.
   Ⓐ universe
   Ⓑ zodiac
   Ⓒ celestial sphere

2. A pattern of stars that seems to be a picture in the sky is called a _____.
   Ⓐ Sun
   Ⓑ ecliptic
   Ⓒ constellation

3. Many stars appear to rise in the east and set in the west, but the North Star remains above the horizon because it is _____.
   Ⓐ fixed
   Ⓑ circumpolar
   Ⓒ a constellation

4. The star that is nearest to the Earth is the _____.
   Ⓐ zodiac
   Ⓑ North Star
   Ⓒ Sun

The Stars Shine

Like all stars, the Sun is a glowing globe of hot gas. And, like other stars, the Sun is a source of tremendous energy. Stars release energy in a variety of forms. Light energy makes stars visible from Earth.

Stars release energy as gamma rays, X rays, ultraviolet waves, microwaves, and radio waves, as well as the more obvious heat and light. It is the light, or brightness, of distant stars that makes them visible from Earth. Astronomers use **magnitude** to refer to a star's brightness, although a star's apparent magnitude depends more on its distance from Earth than on its size. Absolute magnitude is a better measure of a star's brightness. Absolute magnitude is a measure of a star's size, mass, color, and temperature.

Since absolute magnitude is a measure of a star's size, mass, color, and temperature, these properties can be used to classify stars. The Sun is average, as stars go, and is classified as a **main sequence star**. Depending on their size and mass, stars go through definite life cycles. Yellow stars such as the Sun start out as nebulas. They become red giants as they use up their hydrogen fuel, and they eventually end up as black dwarfs. More massive stars explode and end up as neutron stars or **black holes**.

Identify and label the steps in the life cycle of a star.

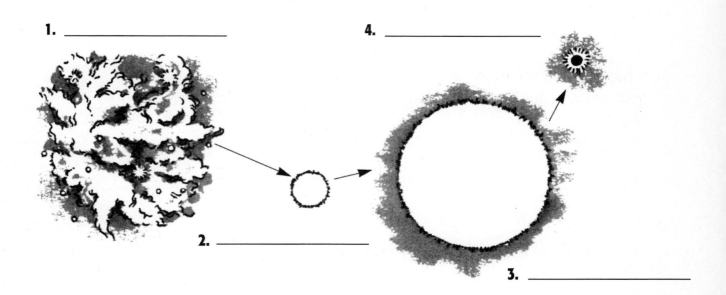

1. _____

2. _____

3. _____

4. _____

Name _____ Date _____

Classifying Stars

To make it easier to compare stars, scientists have developed a way to classify them. The most important factor in how a star is classified is its **spectrum**. The chart shows seven main star types.

STAR CLASSIFICATIONS

Type of Spectrum	Temperature	Example
bluish-white	Over 25,000° C	Velorum
bluish-white	25,000°–10,000° C	Rigel
white	10,000°–8,000° C	Sirius
yellowish-white	7,500°–6,000° C	Canopus
yellow	4,200°–6,000° C	Sun
orange	3,000°–5,000° C	Aldebaran
reddish	2,600° C	Cygni

Answer these questions.

1. What type of spectrum does the Sun have? _____

2. The hottest stars are very rare. What type of spectrum do they have?

   _____

3. What is the temperature range of white stars? _____

4. What is an example of an orange star? _____

5. Which is hotter, Canopus or Sirius? _____

6. Which is cooler, an orange star or a reddish star? _____

7. Does every spectrum group have a different color? _____

8. What are two ways that stars can be classified according to this chart?

   _____

   _____

The Universe

Many scientists hypothesize that 15 billion years ago, all matter in the **universe** was squeezed into a tiny, hot point. Then, suddenly, this matter began to expand outward, as if a giant explosion had occurred. It is still expanding today.

Since distances even within our own galaxy are so great, astronomers measure distances in **light-years**, rather than in astronomical units. (A light-year is the distance light travels in a year.) The Milky Way Galaxy measures about 100,000 light-years from end to end, is about 10,000 light-years across, and contains about 200 billion stars. The closest neighboring galaxy, Andromeda, is about 2.3 million light-years away.

Have you ever wondered if other stars in our galaxy have planets? Astronomers have thought of this possibility for a long time. One star that may have a planet or planets around it is called Barnard's star. Barnard's star is so far away that astronomers could not see a planet there if one existed. But this star seems to wobble in its orbit. This motion could be caused by the pull of one or more planets orbiting it.

Answer these questions.

1. One name for the theory that explains the beginning of the Universe is the Big Bang. Why is this a good name?

_____

_____

2. What is the name of our galaxy? _____

3. Write a sentence that describes what astronomers have observed about Barnard's star.

_____

4. What have scientists inferred from this observation?

_____

5. Imagine that a spacecraft is being sent out of our galaxy toward another spiral galaxy—Andromeda. You have been asked to prepare a package to be sent along in case intelligent beings discover the spacecraft near their planet. Draw and label what you would include in your package. Explain why you selected each item. You should include things that would somehow tell them about our planet, the inhabitants of our planet, our solar system, and our galaxy.

Name _____ Date _____

Telescopes

Most **telescopes** are rather small. These are used mainly by amateur astronomers and students. Some telescopes, however, are very large. These are used mostly by trained scientists.

A **refracting telescope** uses two lenses to gather and focus light. Galileo invented the first refracting telescope in 1609. Sixty years later, Sir Isaac Newton invented the reflecting telescope. A **reflecting telescope** uses mirrors to gather and focus light. Most large telescopes today are reflecting telescopes. A third type is the **radio telescope**. Instead of gathering light waves from space, this type of telescope gathers radio waves.

The largest radio telescope in the world is at Arecibo, Puerto Rico. At Williams Bay, Wisconsin, is the world's largest refracting telescope. The Soviet Union has the largest reflecting telescope. Another large reflecting telescope is located on Palomar Mountain in California.

The map below shows the locations of a few large telescopes in the United States and Puerto Rico. Study the map and then answer the questions.

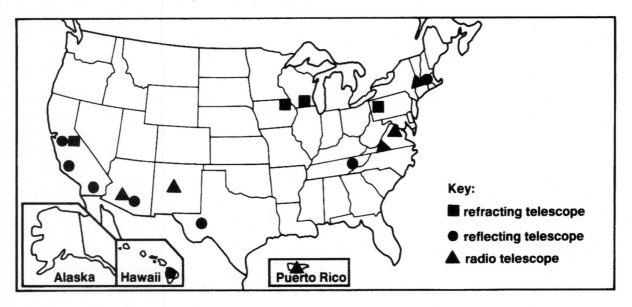

1. How many refracting telescopes are shown? _____

2. How many sites have two kinds of telescopes right near each other? _____

3. What kind of telescope is shown to be on Hawaii? _____

4. How many radio telescopes are shown? _____

5. How many reflecting telescopes are shown? _____

6. Are any of the telescopes shown on the map located in your state? If so, what kind are

   they? _____

Unit 3: Life Science

BACKGROUND INFORMATION

Cells

In the 1600s, Robert Hooke identified and named the cell. All living things are made up of cells, the smallest living units. The cell has all of the properties of a living thing. A cell grows, reproduces, consumes energy, changes it, and excretes waste. Cells react to stimuli and to changes in the environment. Most cells contain a nucleus, cytoplasm, and a cell membrane. Plant cells have, in addition, a cell wall, which is outside of the membrane. The cell wall is made of cellulose and makes the plant cell stiffer than the animal cell. A tree trunk is hard because of the cell walls in the plant cells. The crunch of a carrot or celery is caused by the cell walls breaking as we bite into the food.

The nucleus is the control center of the cell, and it is where the cell begins reproduction. The nucleus contains the chromosomes that determine which hereditary traits are passed on from parents to offspring. The chromosomes are made up primarily of DNA. DNA molecules can duplicate themselves. The cytoplasm is where the special functions of the cell are carried out. The structure and role of the cytoplasm change from one type of cell to another. However, the nucleus (with its DNA) controls what the special function of the cytoplasm will be. The nucleus gives the cytoplasm what it needs to perform its special function. Within the cytoplasm are other structures called organelles. An organelle is any part of a cell with a specific job to do. One of these organelles is the mitochondria. The mitochondria supply the cell with the energy it needs. Other organelles are the ribosomes, the endoplasmic reticulum, and the vacuoles. Ribosomes provide protein. The endoplasmic reticulum carries materials to and from the membrane, and the vacuoles carry food and water throughout the cell. The cell membrane gives the cell its shape and controls what passes into and out of the cell. There are many different types of cells, and each performs specific functions. The human body alone has many different types of cells inside it.

Besides the cell wall, many plant cells have another unique component—chloroplasts. The chloroplasts are small, green bodies shaped like footballs that can be found in the cytoplasm of a plant cell. The chloroplasts give the plant its green color and are vital to the process of photosynthesis. Without the chloroplasts, a plant would not be able to make its own food. Photosynthesis takes place inside the chloroplasts. The parts of a plant that are not green, for example, the bulb of an onion, do not have chloroplasts.

Cell Division

The division of an animal cell differs somewhat from the division of a plant cell. Division of a plant cell (or a cambium cell) begins in the nucleus, as does the division of animal cells. The nucleus becomes two nuclei. But then a new cell wall grows inside the plant cell that divides the cell in two. Then, each new cell grows until it is about the same size as the old cell.

The division of a cell is called mitosis. Before a cell divides, it enters a stage called interphase during which it digests food, uses it for energy, and excretes waste. During this time the cell grows in preparation for division. Different cells divide at different rates, from 15 to 30 minutes to almost two days. The growth of a living thing is caused by the growth and division of its cells.

There are four stages of cell division. The first, prophase, is when the chromosomes in the nucleus become shorter and fatter, then duplicate themselves. The membrane of the nucleus begins to break down. During the second phase, metaphase, the chromosomes line up across the nucleus of the cell. Each chromosome begins to pull apart, separating the duplicated information from the original information. At anaphase, the third phase, the chromosomes pull toward opposite ends of the cell. During the last phase, telophase, cytoplasm is divided, and the nucleus reorganizes into two cells.

Cell Needs

Cells need water, nutrients, and other materials to function. Some of what the cell needs passes in and out of the cell by diffusion, the movement of materials from an area with a lot of the material to an area with less of the material. Water moves across the cell membrane by osmosis. If a cell does not get enough water, or loses more than it takes in, dehydration will occur. When a person sweats, or a plant wilts, water needs to be added to the dehydrated cells.

Biomes

A biome is a large community of plants and animals. Biomes are characterized by the plants and animals that are found there and by the biome's specific climate. There are six major land biomes on Earth. 1. The tropical rain forest is warm and rainy. Its animal life is primarily in the trees. 2. The deciduous rain forests have warm to hot summers and cold winters. The trees there lose their leaves in winter. 3. The boreal forests are very cold and snowy in winter and have very short growing seasons. The trees there are primarily evergreens. 4. The arctic tundra has long, cold winters and cool, short summers. There is not much precipitation. 5. The grasslands have hot, dry summers and cold, snowy winters. 6. The deserts receive very little precipitation. Most are hot year-round, but the nights can be cool because there are no clouds to hold in the warm air.

The Web of Life: Life Cycles, Communities, and Food Chains

All living things go through life cycles. From single-celled organisms to the largest animals, these life cycles include growth, change, consumption of food and water, use of energy, reproduction, and death. Reproduction varies among life forms. Plants reproduce by seeds or spores. Animals may lay eggs or give birth to live young. Some offspring resemble the

parents, and others do not. Some animals, such as frogs, undergo metamorphosis, or a complete change, during their lifetimes. The successful reproduction of a species is important to the population's continued growth or stability.

A typical food chain begins with plants. Most plants make their own food. Algae make their food from nonliving things. Plant cells have chloroplasts, which trap energy from the Sun. Water and carbon dioxide enter the cell through the cell wall. The cell turns the water and gas into food and oxygen. The cell uses the food and passes off the oxygen to be used by other living things. Plants also produce sugar and starch, which are used by other animals. The animals that use plants are herbivores (plant eaters), carnivores (meat eaters who eat the plant eaters), and omnivores (plant and animal eaters). The animals give off carbon dioxide, which is used by the plants. Food webs are used to describe overlapping food chains. These communities and the interactions within them are complex. When their natural order is disrupted, the balance of nature is affected, and organisms can be in danger. The most dire consequence of this disruption is the extinction of a species.

The relationships between organisms in a community can be described in three ways. If the relationship between two organisms is beneficial to both, it is called mutualism. If the relationship helps one organism while the other is neither helped nor harmed, it is called commensalism. If the relationship helps one organism and harms the other, it is known as parasitism.

A community contains food makers, or producers; food takers, or consumers; and decomposers. Typically, the producers are plants. Both other plants and animals eat plants. Carnivores also need plants, as they live off the animals that eat plants. Consumers eat plants, animals, or plants and animals. An animal that eats another animal is a predator. The animal that is eaten is the prey. When the producers and the consumers die, they begin to change; they rot and decay. The decomposers get their food from wastes and dead organisms. Molds, yeast, and bacteria break down the dead matter and give off carbon dioxide. The carbon dioxide is then used by green plants to make food.

The Human Factor

Organisms need to adapt to and change with the changes in their environment to survive. Organisms adapt through physical changes that help them live in their particular habitats and through habits, such as migration, that help them survive. Although many events can disrupt a community and its balance, humans have had the greatest impact upon the Earth's environment. Humans need not only food and energy but also power and space for settlement. Humans create wastes that are not natural to the environment. This environmental pollution is an important concern for everyone. If it is not controlled, the balance of nature is disrupted, organisms die, and those that depend upon the dead organisms may die. It is crucial for humans to find ways to live without creating such disturbances in the environment.

Plant Classification

The plant kingdom contains about 450,000 different kinds of plants, which are each classified into several divisions. The four main classifications for plants are: algae (almost all live in water; from microscopic single-celled plants to seaweed); bryophyta (mosses and liverworts; live in moist places; produce spores); pteridophyta (ferns, clubmosses, horsetails; no flowers); and permatophyta (largest group, with over 350,000 species; reproduce by way of seeds).

Flowering plants are the most numerous type of plant on Earth. They are further classified into groups. Some of the common groups of flowering plants are: grass family (corn, barley, rice, wheat); lily family (violets, hyacinths, tulips, onions, asparagus); palm family (coconut, date); rose family (strawberries, peaches, cherries, apples, and other fruits); legume family (peas, beans, peanuts); beech family; and composite family (sunflowers and others with flowers that are actually many small flowers).

Photosynthesis

Most plants are green. The reason that green plants are green is because they contain chlorophyll, most of which is in the leaves. Chlorophyll is contained in small structures in the leaves called chloroplasts. There are some plants that contain chlorophyll but whose leaves are not green. This is because the chlorophyll has been masked by other pigmentation in the plant. Chlorophyll is necessary for the making of food, but the chlorophyll itself is not used in the food that is made.

Photosynthesis depends on light. A plant that is deprived of light loses its chlorophyll (and its ability to make food) and eventually will die. Plants take in the energy from the Sun and carbon, oxygen, and hydrogen from the air and water. Water and nutrients enter a plant through its roots. Carbon dioxide enters a plant through tiny holes (stomata) in the bottoms of leaves. The plants change these raw materials into carbohydrates and oxygen. The carbohydrates (in the form of a simple sugar called glucose, and starch) are used and stored in the plants for food. The oxygen is released into the air and water where the plants live. In this way, plants constantly replenish the Earth's oxygen supply. Animals breathe the oxygen that plants supply. Animals also supply the carbon dioxide that plants need to survive. This is the oxygen-carbon dioxide cycle.

Green plants are the producers of a community. They not only produce their own food but also are the essential source of food and energy for all communities.

Animal Classification

The animal kingdom can be classified into two large groups: the vertebrates (those with backbones) and the invertebrates (those without backbones). The backbone supports the body and provides flexibility. The spinal cord extends from the brain through the backbone, or spine. Individual nerves branch out from the spinal cord to different parts of the body. Messages from the brain are sent throughout the body through the spinal cord.

Some animals without backbones are sponges, jellyfish, clams, worms, insects, and spiders. Some of these animals have networks of nerves throughout their bodies with no central nerve cords. Many, like insects, have hard exoskeletons that protect their bodies and give them shape.

Adaptation to the Environment

Animals live in almost every type of environment on Earth. Each kind of animal has become well suited to its environment through generations of adaptation. Those animals that are not suited to the environment, or that are poorly adapted, do not survive. The animals that are most fit for their environments continue to reproduce and make others like themselves. Most animals are suited to either land or water life. An obvious adaptation for fish is the gills that allow them to breathe in the water. Lungs allow land animals to breathe in air.

Every part of an animal helps it to live in its particular environment. Some animals are colored in ways that help them to blend into their environments. They are camouflaged to protect them from their enemies. Other animals are brightly colored to attract mates, which helps them with the continuation of their species. Animals' mouths and teeth are adapted to the types of food that they eat. Meat-eating animals have sharp teeth for tearing and ripping their prey, and other teeth for chewing the meat. Animals that eat leaves and grasses have large flat teeth for chewing.

Reproduction

All living things have a life cycle within which they take in food and gases, metabolize, excrete waste, reproduce, and die. If living things fail to reproduce or to create healthy offspring, their species will die out. Animals reproduce in different ways. Some lay eggs, and others give birth to live young. Some offspring look like their parents while others do not. Most reptiles, amphibians, fish, and insects lay eggs. The young of many of these animals can move about and find food for themselves soon after they hatch. Birds also lay eggs, but the adult birds remain with the eggs and care for the young until they can find their own food. Most mammals bear live young. The young are fed milk from the body. Mammals spend more time than other animals feeding, protecting, and teaching their young to survive on their own. Animals that give birth to live young have fewer offspring than those that do not tend to their young. The young of human beings require more care from their parents than any other animal.

The life cycles of some animals include a metamorphosis. A metamorphosis is a complete change in the appearance of an animal. The most striking metamorphosis is the change from caterpillar to butterfly.

Health

Health for children revolves around healthy foods, plenty of exercise, and good hygiene. As children grow, they should begin to recognize that they can make choices that will help them live healthy lives. They need to learn the connections between what they eat and the way they look and feel. They need to have the basic information that will help them to make good food choices. Children need to know that it is never too early to begin healthy habits in eating, exercise, and hygiene. The habits they form now will affect their lives for many years to come.

The Human Body

The cell is the first level of organization in the human body. Groups of cells that have the same structure are called tissues. An organ is a group of different kinds of tissues working together to do a job. A system is a group of organs working together to do a job.

The human body has ten systems: Circulatory System: transports materials to all parts of the body; Muscular System: makes the body move; Endocrine System: regulates growth and development, helps control some body functions; Skeletal System: gives the body shape and support, protects inner organs; Integumentary System: skin, hair, and nails protect the body; Reproductive System: enables adults to produce offspring; Respiratory System: takes in oxygen and releases carbon dioxide; Digestive System: breaks down food into nutrients for cells to use; Excretory System: removes waste produced by cells; Nervous System: controls the body and helps it respond to the environment.

The Five Senses and the Nervous System

The human body collects information using the five senses: sight, smell, hearing, taste, and touch. The nervous system enables us to put all of our senses together so that messages are sent to the brain and we are able to act according to the information that the brain receives. The nervous system enables us to react. It controls all of the other systems in the body.

The major organ of the nervous system is the brain. Another part of the nervous system is a system of nerves that carry information to the brain. The third part of the nervous system is the sense organs. The nose is the sense organ for the sense of smell. There are many nerve cells in the nose that take the information regarding odors to a main nerve called the olfactory nerve. The olfactory nerve carries the information to your brain. Your brain will then tell your body what to do with the information.

Muscles, Bones, and Joints

The human body has more than 600 muscles. Muscles enable us to move, keep some organs moving, and connect bones and skin together. Our muscles keep our blood moving, help us to digest, and keep our lungs expanding and contracting.

Some muscle movements are voluntary, and some are involuntary. Most voluntary muscles are connected to bones. (Tendons are tough cords that connect muscles to bones when they are not directly connected.) When you want to move your arm, you move your biceps and triceps. These muscles contract, and your arm moves. A sheet of muscles under your lungs moves in and out without your conscious effort. These muscles make up the diaphragm. The movement of the diaphragm causes air to rush in and out of your lungs. This movement is involuntary. Some muscle movements are not wholly voluntary or involuntary. Can you control the blinking of your eyes? If you try to stop blinking altogether, you will see that you do not have complete control. Your eye will blink.

When you decide you want to move, a message is sent to your brain. Your brain sends a message to the appropriate muscle to contract. The muscle shortens and becomes firm, and the movement occurs. When you want to stop the movement, your brain tells the muscle to relax. People who are physically fit have muscles that are never fully relaxed. They are always slightly flexed and firm. This is called muscle tone. To get muscle tone, large amounts of blood need to be supplied to the muscle cells. In order to get the blood to the muscle cells, a person must exercise. Muscles that do not get the necessary blood, or that do not get used enough, become weak and soft.

There are three kinds of muscle cells: smooth, cardiac, and skeletal. The smooth muscle cells are long and thin, and they are pointed at each end. They have one nucleus. An example of a smooth muscle is a stomach muscle. Cardiac muscles control the heart. The cardiac muscle cells branch out and weave together. They also have one nucleus. The skeletal muscle cells resemble straws and have many nuclei. The tongue and lips contain skeletal muscles.

There are 206 bones in the human skeletal system that support, protect, and move the body. Bones also produce blood cells in their marrow. The marrow is in the hollowed center of the bone. In young people, all bones have red, blood-producing marrow. Older people have red marrow only in the flat bones, such as the ribs. The other bones contain yellow marrow that does not produce blood cells. Cartilage is a soft, rubbery substance that is found where some bones meet. It keeps the bones from rubbing together. You have cartilage at the end of your nose, too.

Bones join in three ways. A hinge joint allows the bone to move back and forth, as the knees and elbows do. A ball-and-socket joint, such as the shoulder joint, allows the body to move in many directions. A ball-shaped bone fits into the hollow of another bone. Pivot joints, like the one that joins the head to the spine, allow the bones to move around and back. Ligaments, strong bands of material that hold the bones in place, join bones at movable joints.

Blood

Adults have about five liters of blood in their body. Children have about four liters of blood. Blood is a tissue that is more than half liquid. The liquid part of blood is called plasma. Plasma is mostly water. Red blood cells, white blood cells, and platelets float in the plasma.

Red blood cells make up about half of the blood, and the white blood cells and platelets make up the rest. Red blood cells, which resemble tiny flattened balls, carry oxygen from the lungs to the body tissues, and take carbon dioxide from the tissues to the lungs. They are red because they contain a substance called hemoglobin. White blood cells, which are larger than red blood cells and irregular in shape, help fight off disease. After the protective covering cells of the skin, hair, and mucous, white blood cells are the body's second line of defense. If bacteria enter the body, white blood cells move toward them and "swallow" them. (The bacteria then leave the body in pus.) Platelets are important in the clotting of blood when the body is injured.

Hygiene

Keeping the body clean is an important part of staying healthy. Children need to know that when they wash, they are washing off viruses and bacteria, or germs, which can cause illness. Washing the hair and body regularly prevents bacteria from entering the skin through cuts and from getting into the mouth. Hands should always be washed after handling garbage or using the bathroom. Germs can also come from other people. Children should be discouraged from sharing straws, cups, or other utensils. They should be reminded always to cover their mouths when they sneeze or cough, and to use tissues frequently. Children also need to be reminded not to share combs or hats.

RELATED READING

- *Butternut Hollow Pond* by Brian J. Heinz (Millbrook Press, 2000).

- *Dinosaur Parents, Dinosaur Young: Uncovering the Mystery of Dinosaur Families* by Kathleen Weidner Zoehfeld (Clarion, 2001).

- *The Elephant Book: For the Elefriends Campaign* by Ian Redmond (Candlewick Press, 2001).

- *The Forest in the Clouds* by Sneed B. Collard (Charlesbridge, 2000).

- *The Heart: Our Circulatory System* by Seymour Simon (Morrow, 1996).

- *The Human Body: A Photographic Journey Through the Human Body* by Richard Walker (DK Publishing, 2001).

- *I Want to Be an Environmentalist* by Stephanie Maze (I Want to Be Series, Harcourt, 2000).

- *Rain Forest Series* (Raintree Steck-Vaughn, 2003).

- *Scientists of the Biomes Series* (Raintree Steck-Vaughn, 2002).

- *Sea Critters* by Sylvia Earle (National Geographic Society, 2000).

- *The Spirit of the Maasai Man* by Laura Berkeley (Barefoot Books, 2000).

- *Yikes! Your Body, Up Close!* by Mike Janulewicz (Simon & Schuster, 1997).

Unit 3 Assessment

Match the terms at the right with the definitions at the left. Write the letter of the correct term on the line.

_____ 1. structures in the nucleus of a cell that contain the instructions that enable the nucleus to control the activities of the cell

_____ 2. organelles that produce the energy a cell needs

_____ 3. a protective covering around a cell

_____ 4. the control center of a cell

_____ 5. any cell structure that has a specific job to do

_____ 6. the diffusion of water through a cell membrane

a. cell membrane

b. chromosomes

c. mitochondria

d. organelle

e. osmosis

f. nucleus

Use words from the box to complete the sentences.

cold-blooded	warm-blooded	bones	invertebrates	food chain	arthropods

7. Most birds have hollow _____.

8. A _____ shows how organisms depend upon each other for food.

9. Animals whose body temperature changes with that of the surrounding water or air are _____.

10. Animals without backbones are called _____.

11. Animals whose body temperature remains steady are _____.

12. Insects are the largest part of a group of animals called _____.

GO ON TO THE NEXT PAGE ☞

Unit 3 Assessment, p. 2

Choose the correct words from the box to complete the paragraphs. Write the number in the space next to each word to indicate where it belongs.

____ tissue	____ germs	____ system	____ hygiene
____ involuntary	____ exercise	____ toned	____ blood
____ joints	____ circulatory	____ flossing	____ Red
____ cell	____ White	____ voluntary	____ organ
____ muscles	____ brushing	____ lungs	____ systems
____ brain	____ bones	____ respiratory	____ senses
	____ nervous	____ carbon dioxide	

The (1) is the basic building block of all living things. Groups of cells that have the same structure and do the same job are called (2). An (3) is a group of tissues working together to do a specific job. A (4) is a group of organs working together to do a job. There are ten (5) in the human body. The (6) system controls all the other systems in the body.

We have five (7) that we use to collect information from the world around us. The information that we collect is sent to the (8), which in turn sends messages to the body telling it what to do.

Our (9) give us support, our (10) make our bodies move, and (11) allow our bones to bend. We need to (12) our body in order to keep our muscles firm, or (13). Exercise sends (14) to the muscle cells. Some muscles are (15) muscles. We do not think about moving them, but they move anyway. Others are (16) muscles. We can move them when we want to.

The (17) system and the (18) system work together to bring oxygen and nutrients to the cells of the body. Oxygen is collected in the (19). The cells get rid of (20) there, too. (21) blood cells carry oxygen and nutrients to the other cells in the body. (22) blood cells fight infection.

Along with exercise, we need to practice good (23) to stay healthy. This means (24) and (25) our teeth and keeping our body clean. We also need to prevent the spread of (26) from one person to another. We need to take good care of our body so that it will last a long time!

Name _____   Date _____

Cells

Robert Hooke, working with a microscope and some cork in the 1600s, was the first scientist to identify and name the basic unit of living things, the **cell**. Hooke's discovery led to the development of the cell theory, with its three parts. First, all living things are made up of cells. Second, the cell is the smallest unit of structure and function in all living things. Third, all cells can reproduce to form new cells.

Although cells are the basic units of living things, they are made up of many parts, each with a specific function. All cells are surrounded by a **cell membrane** that controls what goes into and out of the cell. The **nucleus** is the command center of a cell. It controls everything that goes on inside the cell. Between the cell membrane and the nucleus is a thick liquid called the **cytoplasm**. Suspended within the cytoplasm are other structures called organelles. An **organelle** is any cell structure with a specific job to do. For example, mitochondria supply a cell with the energy it needs.

Label the cell parts on the diagram below.

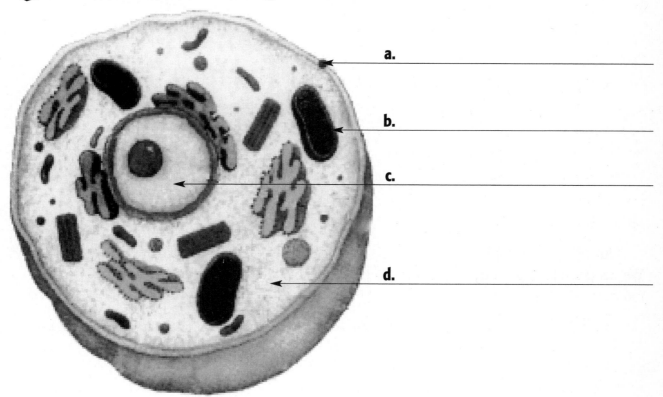

a. _____

b. _____

c. _____

d. _____

Answer these questions on another sheet of paper.

1. Who was the first person to use the term *cell*?
2. In what material did he first see cells?
3. What are the three parts of the cell theory?

Plant and Animal Cells

Plant cells are different from animal cells. Plant cells have a **cell wall** that makes the plant cell stiffer than an animal cell. Plant cells also have small, green bodies shaped like footballs in the cytoplasm. These are **chloroplasts**. Chloroplasts are responsible for photosynthesis. Without chloroplasts, plant cells could not make their own food.

Look at the pictures. Write the letter or letters next to the term that matches each cell part.

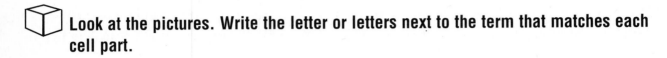

____ cell membrane   ____ cytoplasm   ____ cell wall   ____ chloroplasts   ____ nucleus

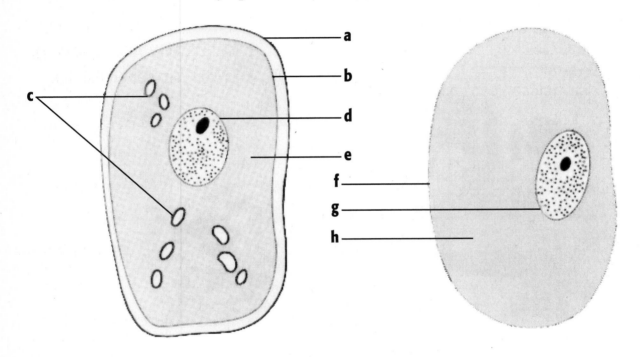

Answer these questions.

1. Which two parts are found only in plant cells? _____

2. In what cell parts does photosynthesis take place? _____

3. What part of a plant keeps the plant stiff? _____

4. What cell part allows only certain substances to diffuse into and out of the cell?

_____

5. Which cell is a plant cell? _____

How Do Cells Work?

Cells need water, nutrients, and other materials to function. Some materials move into and out of cells by **diffusion**, the movement of materials from an area with a lot of the material to an area with less of the material. Water moves across cell membranes by a kind of diffusion called **osmosis**. If a cell loses more water than it takes in, dehydration occurs.

Cell organelles are any part of a cell with a specific function. Within the nucleus of a cell are thin strands called **chromosomes**, which contain the instructions for controlling all functions of the cell. Before a cell divides, it makes an exact copy of the chromosomes. During cell division, the chromosomes and the cytoplasm of the cell divide so that each new cell receives a full set of chromosomes and half the cytoplasm of the original cell.

Complete each sentence with one of the following terms about cells: *organelles, diffusion, osmosis, chromosomes, dehydration.* **Write your answer on the line.**

1. _____ is the movement of materials from an area with a lot of the material to an area with less of the material.

2. _____ happens when cells lose more water than they take in.

3. _____ is the diffusion of water through a cell membrane.

4. Cell _____ are any part of a cell with a special function.

5. _____ are thin strands within the nucleus of a cell.

Answer these questions.

6. Explain what you think happens to the cells of your body if you sweat a lot but do not drink enough water.

_____

_____

7. Explain what happens when you water a wilted plant.

_____

_____

Biomes

A **biome** is a large community of plants and animals. The type of biome is determined by climate and the kinds of plants found there. There are six major land biomes in the world.

Tropical rain forests grow where the climate is warm and rainy. Most of the animal life is found in the trees. Rain forests are important because they produce oxygen, which supports life.

Deciduous forests have warm or hot summers and cold winters. Deciduous trees lose their leaves every fall. Deer, squirrels, foxes, owls, and snakes are found in deciduous forests.

Boreal forests grow in places with very cold, snowy winters and short growing seasons. The trees are mostly evergreens. In this type of forest you will find deer, bears, snowshoe hares, and beavers.

On the **arctic tundra**, the winters are long and cold, and the summers are short and cool. Animals on the tundra, such as the snowy owl, are adapted for cold weather. They also blend in with the snow.

Grasslands have winters that are cold and snowy and summers that are hot and dry. Many small animals, such as ground squirrels, prairie dogs, and many kinds of birds, are found in the grasslands.

Because **deserts** receive very little rainfall, the plants there are far apart so they don't compete with each other for moisture. The desert supports many animals, such as mice, snakes, and coyotes.

 Complete the chart by using words from the reading selection.

BIOME	DESCRIPTION
	1. long, cold winters; animals blend in with snow
	2. warm summers, cold winters; trees lose leaves
	3. receive little rainfall; plants are far apart
	4. cold, snowy winters; evergreen trees
	5. hot, dry summers; home to prairie dogs
	6. warm and rainy; produces much oxygen

Comparing Biomes

A biome is a large community of plants and animals. Biomes are characterized by the plants and animals found there and by a specific type of climate. Different parts of the world with the same type of biome may have very similar climates. For example, most deserts are extremely dry and have very little rainfall, no matter where they are located.

Look at the following bar graph to find the amount of precipitation each biome receives annually.

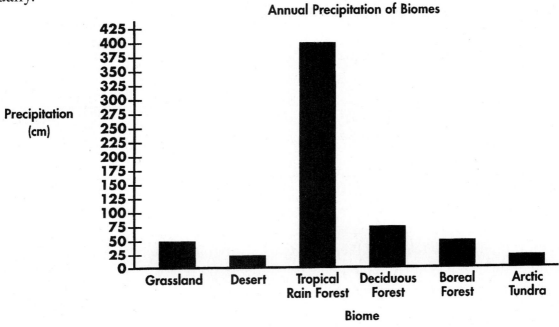

Answer these questions.

1. Write the amount of precipitation next to the name of each biome.

   _____ Grassland   _____ Deciduous forest

   _____ Desert   _____ Boreal forest

   _____ Tropical rain forest   _____ Arctic tundra

2. Which biome has the greatest amount of rainfall in a year? the least amount of rainfall?

   _____

3. Which biome—deciduous forest or boreal forest—receives more rainfall?

   _____

   _____

4. Deserts receive very little rainfall. What kinds of plants and animals do you think could

   live in a desert biome? _____

   _____

Classifying Plants

Green plants provide the air with something you need—oxygen. They also use the carbon dioxide that you exhale when they produce food. This relationship between you and plants is called the **oxygen-carbon dioxide cycle**.

Below are the steps of the oxygen-carbon dioxide cycle. In each step, the words have been scrambled. Put the words in their proper order.

1. in oxygen animals breathe

_____

2. breathe out dioxide carbon animals

_____

3. carbon dioxide in plants take

_____

4. own chlorophyll make food and their plants use carbon dioxide water sunlight to

_____

_____

5. off oxygen plants give

_____

Scientists sometimes summarize their observations by making a diagram. In the space below, make a diagram that shows the five steps in the oxygen-carbon dioxide cycle.

Plant Reproduction

Reproduction is the method by which living things make more of their own kind. There are several ways that plants reproduce.

Mosses are small plants with no real roots, leaves, or stems. Growing in moist, shady places, mosses get the water and nutrients they need by living close to the soil and passing the food and water slowly from cell to cell. Mosses reproduce by **spores**. Spores are special cells that can develop into new plants like the plants that made them.

Ferns also grow in moist, shady places. Ferns have roots, stems, and leaves, however, and can grow very large. Ferns also reproduce by spores. The spores grow on the underside of the fern leaves. When the tiny pockets of spores break open, thousands of spores float away on the wind to begin new ferns.

Gymnosperms are seed-bearing plants that produce seeds in **cones**. Fir trees are common gymnosperms. When the seeds are ready, the cones release them into the wind. When the seeds come to rest in the right kind of soil, they will begin to grow a new plant.

Angiosperms are seed-bearing plants that are also called flowering plants. They are the most common type of plant. All flowering plants and trees are angiosperms. Grass, flowers, and fruit trees all produce seeds. Each seed contains a tiny plant and stored food to help it grow.

 Answer these questions.

1. What kind of plant is a pine tree? _____

2. How would a pine tree reproduce? _____

3. What is the most common type of plant? _____

4. What is in a flower seed? _____

5. What is a spore? _____

Food for Growth

You need to eat every day. Food gives you energy. It also provides you with the materials you need to grow and repair body tissue. Plants need food for the same reasons. You can see how a bean seed uses some of its stored food.

You will need

- ★ 4 bean seeds
- ★ water
- ★ soil
- ★ paper cup (plastic-coated)
- ★ aluminum foil

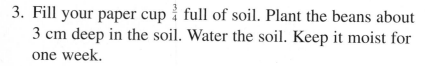

1. Soak the bean seeds in water overnight. Then, look at them. Describe them. How do they feel?

   _____

   _____

2. Wrap one bean tightly in a small piece of aluminum foil. Make sure the foil covers the bean completely so that no water or air can reach it.

3. Fill your paper cup $\frac{3}{4}$ full of soil. Plant the beans about 3 cm deep in the soil. Water the soil. Keep it moist for one week.

4. Dig up the bean seeds. How do the unwrapped beans look? _____

   How do they feel? _____

   What other changes have occurred? _____

   Where did the food come from for these changes? _____

5. Unwrap the bean in aluminum foil. How is it different from the other beans?

   _____

With the right conditions, a bean seed will use its stored food to grow a new plant. If the bean has no oxygen or water, however, it cannot use the stored food.

Food Chains

There are two types of **plankton**: animal and plant. Plant plankton captures light energy from the Sun and converts it to food. Most animals in the sea, including animal plankton, ultimately depend upon plant plankton for food. All these tiny plants use only a half percent of the light energy that strikes the surface of the ocean. Yet they help feed an ocean full of animals!

A **food chain** shows how animals depend on other organisms for food. Most ocean food chains begin with plant plankton. Most land food chains begin with plants, also.

 **Study the following food chain. Then, answer the questions.**

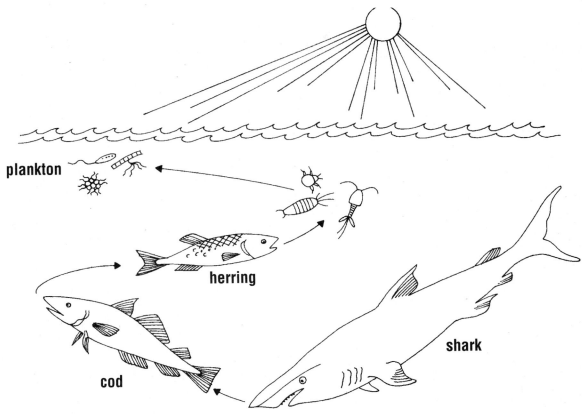

plankton

herring

cod

shark

1. What does the cod eat? _____

2. What eats the cod? _____

3. Where does the energy for this food chain come from? _____

4. What is the smallest organism in this food chain? _____

5. What would happen if all plant plankton suddenly disappeared? _____

_____

_____

Backbone or No Backbone

Animals are often divided into two categories: those with backbones and those without backbones. Animals with backbones are called **vertebrates**. Animals without backbones are called **invertebrates**.

Vertebrates have an internal **skeleton**, or a skeleton inside the body. The skeleton is usually made of bone, but in some cases, as in the shark, the backbone is made of cartilage. Cartilage is a tough, rubbery gristle. Fishes, amphibians, reptiles, birds, and mammals are all vertebrates.

Many invertebrates have an **exoskeleton**, or a skeleton outside of their body. An exoskeleton is very strong, but it cannot grow with the body. The exoskeleton has to be shed when the body grows. Insects are the largest groups of invertebrates. Other invertebrates are snails, jellyfish, worms, sponges, crabs, and lobsters.

📦 **Write the names from the box under the correct heading.**

Invertebrates   **Vertebrates**

_____   _____

_____   _____

_____   _____

_____   _____

_____   _____

_____   _____

_____   _____

_____   _____

_____   _____

_____   _____

starfish	ant
turtle	frog
lobster	horse
spider	mouse
jellyfish	dog
worm	bear
sponge	eagle
beetle	fish
lizard	bee
snail	crab
shrimp	rabbit
human	snake

Kinds of Animals

Mammals are covered in fur or hair. They give birth to live young and feed them milk from their bodies. They are warm-blooded. This means that they can maintain a warm body temperature in cold weather. Mammals all have backbones, and they can be found all over the Earth.

Amphibians are animals that can live both on land and in water. Most breed in the water and lay eggs. The eggs develop into tadpoles and then adults. Amphibians can be found everywhere except Antarctica and Greenland.

Reptiles are scaly-skinned animals. Some live in water, and some live on land. Reptiles are cold-blooded. They control their body temperature by the sunlight. If they need heat, they sit in the sunlight. If they are too warm, they move to the shade. Most reptiles are found in warm areas of the world.

Birds are the only creatures with feathers. They are warm-blooded animals. Most birds can fly, but some, such as the ostrich, cannot.

Fish are streamlined for swimming. They have a strong tail, and they have fins for balance and steering. Fish absorb oxygen from the water with their gills.

Arthropods are animals without backbones. They have jointed legs, a segmented body, and an exoskeleton. Insects are the largest group of arthropods.

Use a science book, an encyclopedia, or what you already know to find pictures of each type of animal. Write the following headings on a piece of poster board, and paste your pictures under the correct headings.

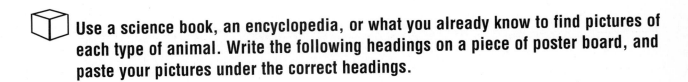

Mammals   **Amphibians**   **Reptiles**   **Birds**   **Fish**   **Arthropods**

Life Cycles

You have learned that animals and plants go through a **life cycle**. A cycle is a period of time in which plants and animals are born, live, reproduce, and die. The word *cycle* comes from the word that meant *wheel* to the ancient Romans and Greeks. A cycle in nature is like the rim of the wheel. If you start at one point of the rim and go around the wheel, you come back to the point from which you started. The frog is an amphibian that has an interesting life cycle.

Look at the pictures. Each one shows a different stage in the growth of a frog, from egg to adult. Read about each stage. Then, match each stage with the right picture. Write the correct number on the line next to each picture.

1. The egg, covered by a jellylike substance, is fertilized.
2. The egg cell divides to make two cells.
3. The cells divide again and again. A ball of cells forms.
4. The embryo changes shape. The head and tail form. The egg hatches. Gills develop and are used for breathing. The embryo is now a tadpole.
5. The tadpole grows bigger. A flap of skin grows over the gills. The hind legs develop.
6. The front legs appear. The tail gets shorter. Lungs form for breathing. The gills disappear.
7. The tail disappears. The tadpole becomes a frog that can live on land.

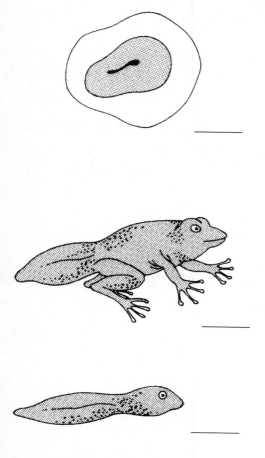

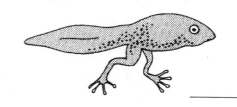

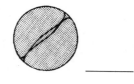

Reptiles and Birds

How would you like to have this creature for a pet? Sorry, this animal isn't around anymore. Its name was Tyrannosaurus. Tyrannosaurus was 15 m (about 50 ft) long and $5\frac{1}{2}$ m (about 18 ft) tall. Scientists have found many fossil remains of Tyrannosaurus. They have concluded that Tyrannosaurus was a reptile.

 Describe the characteristics that this animal had that led scientists to reach this conclusion. Use a reference book if you need help.

1. Was it warm-blooded or cold-blooded? _____

2. How did it reproduce? _____

3. What kind of skin did it have? _____

4. Tyrannosaurus could live entirely on land. What characteristics that you named above

   helped it do this? _____

Below are drawings of two interesting animals. One is an extinct flying reptile called Pteranodon. It probably lived about 200 million years ago. A portion of its skin stretched across bone to form a wing. It also had hollow bones that made it lighter. The other drawing shows a modern bird that is in danger of becoming extinct. It is a California condor.

Compare the characteristics of the two animals. Write each animal's characteristics on another sheet of paper. Use a reference book if you need help.

condor

pteranodon

Birds

Birds are the only animals that have feathers. This body covering is actually a special kind of scale. Feathers provide insulation. They keep birds from losing too much body heat on cold days.

Because they have hollow bones, birds are very lightweight. This makes it easier for them to fly. They also have a very large breastbone in their skeleton. The powerful muscles that move the wings are attached to it.

Their brains, called eye brains, have well-developed areas that deal with sight. Even when they are high in the sky, birds can see things on the ground quite clearly. However, birds do not have a good sense of smell. This is because the areas of their eye brains connected with the sense of smell are poorly developed.

When in flight, the body of a bird uses a lot of energy and gives off a lot of heat. To cool themselves, these animals have an internal "air-conditioning system." It is made up of a network of air sacs that are connected to the lungs. When a bird's body temperature gets too high, cooling air flows through its air sacs.

Match each sentence with the correct body part. Write the letter of the body part on the line before the sentence.

_____ 1. These cover the body of a bird.

_____ 2. These kinds of brains are well-developed in areas to do with sight.

_____ 3. These help keep birds very light in weight.

_____ 4. Powerful wing muscles are attached to this large bone.

_____ 5. These help cool a bird during flight.

a. breastbone

b. air sacs

c. feathers

d. hollow bones

e. eye brains

Mammals

The mouse and the chimpanzee are different animals. But they are both **mammals**.

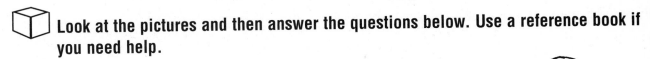

Look at the pictures and then answer the questions below. Use a reference book if you need help.

1. Compare the location of the eyes for each of the two mammals.

   _____

   _____

2. Which of the two mammals has the better ability to chew

   through objects? _____

3. Which of the two mammals has the better ability to

   hold objects?_____

4. With what group of animals should the mouse be classified?

   _____

5. With what group of mammals should the chimpanzee be

   classified? _____

All mammals live and grow in their mother's body before they are born. This is called the **gestation period**. The amount of time they develop in the mother's body is different for different mammals. The gestation period for different mammals is shown in the chart.

Use the information in the chart to make a graph that shows these differences. Use another sheet of paper to make your graph.

Opossum	12 days	Pig	10 weeks
Hamster	16 days	Cow	9 months
Mouse	21 days	Chimpanzee	9 months
Rabbit	30 days	Human	9 months
Cat	9 weeks	Horse	11 months
Dog	9 weeks	Elephant	18–21 months

Study your graph. Then, make some predictions about the length of time some other animals remain in their mother's body. Do library research to compare your predictions with the actual lengths of time.

The Web of Life

The biosphere includes the atmosphere, the Earth's crust, the oceans, and all the life that exists there. The Sun is also considered part of the biosphere. Its energy enters the atmosphere and is important to life in the biosphere.

Within the biosphere are many different **populations** of animals and plants. Populations interact with other populations and nonliving things in their environments. Groups of populations living together form **communities**. The populations within these communities form food chains. These populations depend upon each other for their survival. The food chains create a balance in the community.

Here is an example. In a forest community, there are different populations. There are grasses, rabbits, and foxes. The rabbits eat the grasses. The foxes eat the rabbits. If there were no foxes, the rabbit population could grow too quickly. They would use up all the grasses. Then, the rabbits would begin to die because there would not be enough grasses. If there were no rabbits in the community, the foxes would die. They could not live on the grasses in the woods. Because there are **predators** and **prey** in the community, the community stays balanced.

Every community has three types of organisms. There are **producers**, **consumers**, and **decomposers**. The producers are usually plants. The consumers are usually the animals. Decomposers are molds and bacteria. They break down the dead organisms and return them to the soil. All of these keep the community balanced. If something hurts a population, like a disease, a fire, or pollution, it affects the whole community.

 On another sheet of paper, make a diagram showing a decomposition>producer> consumer cycle. Use the following labels in your diagram.

a. animals and plants die
b. decomposers break down dead organisms
c. materials return to the soil and are used by plants to make new food
d. animals eat plants
e. animals eat animals

Decomposers

Along with plants and animals, decomposers are important to the balance of nature. The decomposers, such as mold and bacteria, break down dead organisms and waste and return them to the soil. Plants then use the soil to grow. This completes the cycle. Where can you find decomposers? What do they need in order to be active? To find out, try this activity.

You will need

* 4 plastic containers
* newspaper
* sand
* marking pen
* potting soil
* water

1. Label the four containers **dry soil**, **damp soil**, **dry sand**, and **damp sand**.

2. Tear four strips of newspaper about 4 cm wide and 12 cm long. Lay each strip in a plastic container, with one end of the strip hanging over the edge.

3. Fill the two containers labeled **dry soil** and **damp soil** with potting soil. Fill the other two containers with clean sand. One end of the strip of newspaper should stick out of the soil or sand in each container.

4. Add a little water to the containers labeled **damp soil** and **damp sand**. Add water to the containers every few days to keep the soil and sand damp.

5. Observe the condition of the strips of newspaper in the containers for one week. Record your observations in the chart.

Day	Dry Soil	Damp Soil	Dry Sand	Damp Sand
1				
2				
3				
4				
5				
6				
7				

GO ON TO THE NEXT PAGE ☞

Decomposers, p. 2

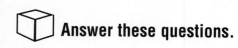 **Answer these questions.**

1. In what container did the strip of newspaper decompose the most? Explain why you think this happened.

   _____

   _____

   _____

2. What happened to the strip of newspaper in the containers that were kept dry? Explain why you think this happened.

   _____

   _____

   _____

3. What could account for the difference in decomposition in the container with the damp soil and the one with the damp sand?

   _____

   _____

   _____

4. How do decomposers help the environment?

   _____

   _____

5. Add arrows to the diagram below to show how energy flows through a food web.

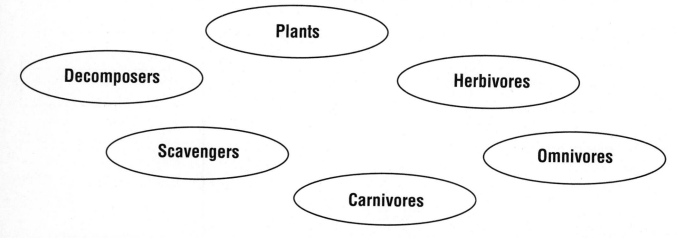

Pollution

When we hear the word *pollution*, most of us think of either water pollution or air pollution. But there are many other types of pollution. The most visible type is solid-waste pollution. This includes anything from trash along the highway to junked cars and old tires. Anything solid that you throw away, such as an old comic book or the leftovers from your lunch, is solid waste. Any waste that harms the environment is a form of pollution.

The United States produces about two billion tons of solid waste each year. That's about 20 kg of solid waste for each person each day! Think about how much waste that is—about half your body mass.

What can we do about solid waste? The good news is that with a little effort, we can cut down on pollution. We can **recycle**.

Think about an aluminum can. You can throw it away, or you can recycle it. When you throw it away, it will probably be taken with the rest of your garbage to a landfill. The smell of a landfill pollutes the air. In some cases, materials in the landfill leak down through the soil and pollute underground water.

Think a little more about the aluminum can. If you recycle it, you won't be adding it to an overfilled landfill. But just as important as that, reusing aluminum means saving natural resources and saving energy. Any aluminum that is recycled will not need to be mined from the ground. Energy that would be needed to process new aluminum ore will be saved.

In the last few years, many communities have started recycling aluminum cans, glass bottles and jars, and newspapers. Some communities have also begun to recycle other waste, such as tin-covered steel cans and plastic containers. Each item that is recycled saves energy and doesn't add to solid-waste pollution. You can help. Find out how much you and your family can recycle.

You will need

☆ paper grocery bags   ☆ marking pen   ☆ trash

1. Keep track of all the things you can recycle in one week. Before you throw something away, think about whether it could be recycled.

2. Organize your recycling. Label a paper grocery bag for each type of item that can be recycled. You should have one bag for each of the following: newspapers; magazines and junk mail; cardboard; glass; aluminum and tin; and plastic.

GO ON TO THE NEXT PAGE 👉

Pollution, p. 2

3. Ask your family to help by putting anything that can be recycled into the right bag.

4. At the end of the week, fill out the following chart to find out how much you recycled. Count the number of cans and bottles in each category. For the paper and cardboard recycling, you can weigh each type if you have a scale. Otherwise, count the number of newspapers, magazines, and cardboard boxes.

5. Most communities recycle some things. Find out whether your community will accept the items you separated for recycling.

Newspaper	Cardboard	Magazines and Junk Mail	Glass	Aluminum and Tin	Plastic

Answer these questions.

1. If recycling is so helpful, why do you think many people do not recycle?

_____

_____

_____

2. What can you do to help prevent solid-waste pollution?

_____

_____

_____

We're Organized

The **cell** is the first of five levels of organization of living things. Groups of cells that have the same structure and do the same job are called **tissues**. The muscle, in your upper arm, your bicep, is an example of a tissue. An **organ** is a group of different kinds of tissues working together to do a specific job. Your heart is an example of an organ. A **system** is a group of organs working together to do a job. Your respiratory system, for example, is responsible for breathing. Your entire body is an example of the highest level of organization: the **organism**.

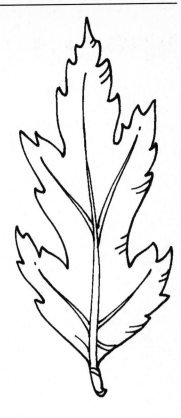

Classify each thing listed below by using one of these terms: *cell, tissue, organ, system, organism.*

_____ **1.** stomach

_____ **2.** blood

_____ **3.** leaf

_____ **4.** digestive

_____ **5.** nerve

_____ **6.** tree bark

_____ **7.** muscle

_____ **8.** lung

_____ **9.** oak tree

_____ **10.** nervous

_____ **11.** liver

_____ **12.** amoeba

_____ **13.** cat

_____ **14.** circulatory

Systems Working Together

Your body has trillions of cells, hundreds of tissues, dozens of organs, and ten systems: skeletal system, muscular system, digestive system, nervous system, excretory system, respiratory system, circulatory system, endocrine system, reproductive system, and integumentary system.

Systems in the body work together to get things done. The digestive system, the circulatory system, and the respiratory system work together to provide your body cells with food and oxygen they need to function. The digestive system turns the food you eat into nutrients that the body can use. At the same time, the respiratory system brings oxygen into the lungs. Oxygen passes from the lungs into the circulatory system, and nutrients pass from the small intestine into the circulatory system. In the circulatory system, the blood carries the oxygen and nutrients to all the cells of the body.

Remember:
- Cells are the basic units of all living things.
- Groups of cells with the same function are called tissues.
- Groups of tissues with the same function are called organs.
- Organs with related functions belong to a system.

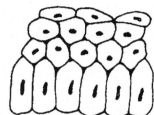

 Match the terms in the box with the definitions. Write the letter of the correct term on the line.

| **a.** cell | **b.** tissues | **c.** organ | **d.** system | **e.** organism | **f.** blood |

_____ **1.** a body structure made of different kinds of tissues that work together to do a specific job

_____ **2.** groups of cells with the same structure and function

_____ **3.** the basic unit of structure and function of an organism

_____ **4.** fluid tissue that moves from place to place

_____ **5.** a living thing that carries out all life functions

_____ **6.** a group of organs that work together to do a job

Answer this question on another sheet of paper.

7. Can you think of another way that the systems of the body work together?

The Digestive System

The **digestion** of food begins in your mouth. Your saliva contains an enzyme that breaks down starches into sugar. From there, the food moves down the esophagus into the stomach. The stomach continues the digestive process and moves the food to the small intestine. You can show that the digestion of starches begins in your mouth.

You will need

★ plain, unsalted soda cracker

★ variety of foods such as bread, unsweetened cereal, peanuts, celery

1. A cracker contains starch. Take a bite of the cracker. How does it taste?

   _____

2. Continue to chew the cracker for one minute.

   How does it taste? _____

   Why does it taste this way? _____

   _____

3. Now test some other foods. How can you find out if they contain starch?

   _____

4. Record your results in the chart below. Compare your results with those of your classmates.

Types of Food	Starch/No Starch
cracker	starch

The Small Intestine

Stomach muscles push partly-digested food into the small intestine. Most of the food still isn't ready to pass out of the small intestine and into the blood vessels. This food must be broken down further until it can dissolve in water. Only then can food diffuse through the walls of the small intestine. You can make a model of the wall of the small intestine to show that only dissolved substances will pass through.

You will need

- ☆ paper towel
- ☆ measuring spoon
- ☆ two clear glasses
- ☆ cinnamon
- ☆ salt
- ☆ warm water
- ☆ funnel

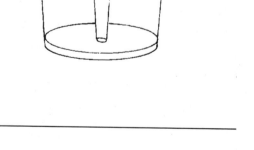

1. Pour water into one glass. Add two teaspoons of salt. Stir until the salt has dissolved.

2. Add two teaspoons of cinnamon. Stir again. Does the cinnamon dissolve?

   _____

3. Fold the paper towel in quarters.

4. Open one side of the paper towel so that it forms a filter. It will act like the wall of the small intestine.

5. Place your filter in the funnel. Place the funnel on top of the empty glass. Pour the mixture through. What remains in the filter?

   _____

6. Taste the water that has been filtered.

   How does it taste? _____

   What passed through the filter? _____

7. What needs to be done in the body to the cinnamon before it can pass through the walls of the small intestine?

   _____

Many foods are like cinnamon. They do not dissolve in water. They must be broken down in the body by digestive juices.

The Circulatory System

The **circulatory system** and the respiratory system work together to bring oxygen and nutrients to the body cells and to remove carbon dioxide from the cells.

To follow the blood through the circulatory system, start in the heart—the right **atrium**, to be exact. As one valve opens, blood that needs oxygen flows from the heart. The valve closes, and another valve opens, allowing the blood to proceed to the lungs. In the lungs, the blood cells get the oxygen they need. They also get rid of carbon dioxide. As red blood cells take in oxygen and give up carbon dioxide, they change in color from dark red to bright red. The blood then leaves the lungs and passes through the heart again, this time through the left ventricle. The heart pumps it through the large arteries into the smaller arteries and capillaries throughout the body. There, oxygen and nutrients are distributed to all the other cells, and wastes are picked up. The blood becomes dark red again. Then, the blood returns to the heart—the right atrium—to begin its trip once more.

The blood is carried away from the heart in blood vessels called **arteries**. The blood returns to the heart in blood vessels called **veins**. The smallest blood vessels, no wider than a hair, are called **capillaries**.

Each time the heart "beats," it pushes blood in two directions at once. Some of the blood goes to the lungs, and some of the blood goes to the rest of the body. If you have ever heard a heartbeat, you know that it makes a "puh-pum" type of sound. The "puh" sound is made when the valves of the heart close and push the blood one way, and the "pum" is the sound of different valves pushing the blood the other way. Each beat of the heart is a double pump. The heart pushes your blood through your body about once every minute.

 Draw a line from the description on the left to the correct term on the right.

1. brings oxygen and nutrients to cells and takes away carbon dioxide
2. bring blood to the heart
3. take blood away from the heart
4. where cells take in oxygen and give up carbon dioxide
5. the smallest blood vessels
6. works with the circulatory system to deliver oxygen to cells
7. blood with little oxygen
8. blood with plenty of oxygen

a. veins

b. capillaries

c. bright red

d. circulatory system

e. dark red

f. arteries

g. respiratory system

h. lungs

Follow That Blood!

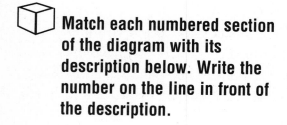 The diagram below shows the circulatory system of the human body. Trace the pathway through which blood flows through the system so that it makes a complete loop, beginning and ending at 1. Use a colored pencil. Then, identify the numbered parts of the circulatory system.

1. _____

2. _____

3. _____

4. _____

5. _____

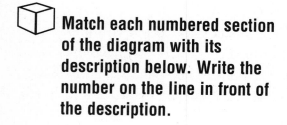 Match each numbered section of the diagram with its description below. Write the number on the line in front of the description.

_____ smallest of all blood vessels

_____ where red blood cells drop off carbon dioxide and pick up oxygen

_____ carries blood away from the heart

_____ pumps blood throughout the body

_____ carries blood to the heart

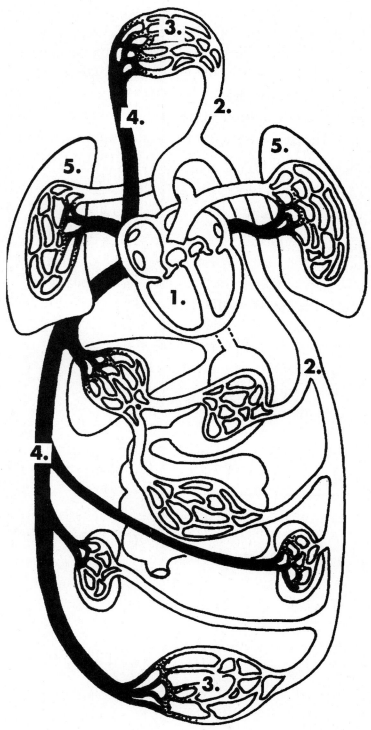

Blood Cells

Red blood cells look like tiny flattened basketballs. Their red color comes from a substance in the cells called **hemoglobin**. Hemoglobin picks up oxygen in the lungs and carries it to all the cells of the body. Sometimes, red blood cells move alone in the blood. At other times, they travel in rows that look like stacks of coins. Red blood cells are made inside bones. Unlike most cells, a red blood cell has no nucleus. Red blood cells live about four months. Old ones are removed by the **white blood cells**. One milliliter of blood has between four million and six million red blood cells. If all the red blood cells from an adult's body were placed side by side, they would go around the Earth four times.

White blood cells look different from red blood cells, and they do different work. They surround and destroy invading bacteria. White blood cells are large and contain nuclei. They have irregular shapes. Some are made in the same bones as the red blood cells. Others are made in special glands. Some white blood cells live only a few days. In one milliliter of blood there are between 5,000 and 10,000 white blood cells. When bacteria enter a person's body, the number increases.

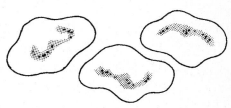

Read each statement. Write *true* or *false* about each statement.

_____ **1.** A red blood cell has a nucleus.

_____ **2.** Red blood cells contain hemoglobin.

_____ **3.** Red blood cells are made inside bones.

_____ **4.** You have more white blood cells than red blood cells.

_____ **5.** White blood cells are larger than red blood cells.

_____ **6.** Red blood cells remove old white blood cells.

_____ **7.** White blood cells look like flattened basketballs.

_____ **8.** Some white blood cells live only a few days.

_____ **9.** One milliliter of blood may have five million red blood cells.

_____ **10.** When bacteria enter your body, the number of white blood cells increases.

www.svschoolsupply.com
© Steck-Vaughn Company

Unit 3: Life Science
Science 5, SV 7937-5

The Respiratory System

The **respiratory system** is responsible for the exchange of gases in the cells of the body. When you inhale, air passes through your nose, down your windpipe, and into two tubes called **bronchial tubes**. These tubes lead into your lungs. The tubes branch many times, like a tree, so that your lungs are filled with tiny tubes. The smallest tubes can only be seen with a microscope. At the ends of these tubes are **air sacs**.

Air is moved from the air sacs into the cells of the body by diffusion. This is the movement of a substance from an area with a lot of that substance to an area with less of that substance. When the oxygen-poor cells arrive in the lungs from the heart, the oxygen moves into the cells. The carbon dioxide, on the other hand, is more concentrated in the cells, so it moves out of the cells and into the air sacs. When you exhale, the carbon dioxide leaves your body by the same path by which the oxygen entered.

Breathing is only a partly voluntary movement. Part of the reason that you breathe is involuntary. It is caused by the movement of muscles called the **diaphragm**. This is a sheet of muscles beneath your lungs. When the diaphragm moves downward, it increases the space around the lungs, causing air to rush into your lungs. When the diaphragm moves up, it decreases the space around your lungs, and the air rushes out.

 Complete this crossword puzzle about the respiratory system.

Across

4. the system that brings oxygen to cells

6. the organ in which the oxygen-carbon dioxide exchange takes place

7. where oxygen goes after it has entered your nose

8. the outside organ that helps you breathe

Down

1. a sheet of muscles below your lungs

2. the type of tubes that leads into your lung

3. the way oxygen gets into cells

5. microscopic pocket of air in the lungs

Respiration Rates

In and out. In and out. Without even having to think about it, you constantly breathe—while you're reading this, while you eat a snack, even while you sleep. With each breath, your body gets the oxygen it needs and gives off carbon dioxide. Find out the number of times you breathe during a day.

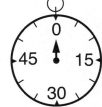

You will need

★ stopwatch, watch, or clock with second hand

★ calculator

1. Work with a partner. Your partner will tell you when to start and will tell you to stop 60 seconds later.

2. Sit very still. When your partner says "go," start counting your breaths. Remember, breathing in once and then breathing out counts as one breath.

3. Write your number of breaths in the space marked *1 minute* in the chart below.

4. Finish filling in the chart below. To find out your number of breaths in an hour, multiply the number of breaths in 1 minute by 60. To find out how often you breathe in a day, multiply the number of breaths in an hour by 24. Multiply that number by 365 to find the number of breaths in a year.

Number Of Breaths			
1 minute	1 hour	1 day	1 year

Answer these questions.

1. Do you think your breathing rate, or how fast you breathe, can change? Explain your response.

_____

_____

2. Test your response to the question above. First, run in place for 30 seconds. Then, repeat steps 1–3. Describe what happens.

_____

_____

The Skeletal System

There are 206 bones in your **skeletal system**. The bones form a frame that gives you support. Many bones protect important parts of your body. Some help you move. However, bones can break or become diseased.

 Each group of drawings and symbols gives you the clues needed to name a type of movable joint. Write its name on the line.

1.

_____

2.

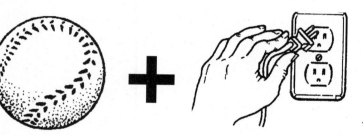

_____

 Complete these exercises.

3. Go to the library and find books and reference material about the symptoms, causes, and treatments of the following diseases or bone injuries:

bursitis	slipped disk	bone fracture
dislocated shoulder	osteomyelitis	bone break
aplastic anemia	arthritis	bone cancer

4. Write a research report that summarizes what you have learned. Your report should include this information:

- causes for the disease or bone injury
- who is likely to get the disease or injury
- how doctors treat the disease or repair the injury

The Muscular System

The **muscular system** produces movement. There are over 600 different muscles in your body. Muscles cover the skeleton. They also line the walls of some organs, such as the heart and stomach. Tendons attach muscles to bone.

Muscles can be voluntary and involuntary. **Voluntary muscles** are the ones that you can control. You can tell them when to move. Most voluntary muscles are attached to bones. **Involuntary muscles**, like those of the heart, move without your having to think about them. The muscles that control your eyelids may seem like voluntary muscles. You can blink your eyes when you want to. However, you cannot keep your eyes from blinking when they need to! You do not have complete control over them.

Muscles cause movement by contracting or getting shorter and firmer. This action pulls on the bones or other body structures. Muscles move the blood through your body. They also move food and wastes through your body.

Muscle tone is achieved through exercise. If a person has good muscle tone, the muscles do not completely relax. They are always slightly contracted. For you to have good muscle tone, plenty of blood needs to reach the muscle cells. This requires exercise.

There are three types of muscles in the body. Each type of muscle cell looks different. The **smooth muscles** are long and thin and pointed at each end. The stomach has smooth muscle cells. **Cardiac muscles** make up the heart. They branch out and weave together. **Skeletal muscles** are long and shaped like cylinders (similar to straws). Unlike the other muscle cells, the skeletal muscle cells have many nuclei. The tongue and lips are skeletal muscles, as are the biceps and triceps in your arms.

Match each description with the correct term. Write the letter of the term on the line before the description.

_____ 1. muscles that make up the heart

_____ 2. muscles over which you have complete control

_____ 3. what muscles do to cause movement

_____ 4. necessary for muscle tone

_____ 5. muscle cells with many nuclei

_____ 6. attach muscles to bone

_____ 7. muscles that move without conscious effort

a. tendons

b. involuntary

c. contract

d. cardiac

e. exercise

f. skeletal

g. voluntary

How Is Your Muscle Tone?

How strong you are depends on your muscle "tone." Good muscle tone means that your muscle cells are well-nourished. Exercising brings blood carrying food to the muscle cells. In this activity, you will measure the strength of some of your muscles. Work with a partner.

You will need

☆ textbook

☆ watch with a second hand

☆ clear desktop

1. Stretch your left arm out on the desktop so the backs of your upper arm, elbow, lower arm, and hand are all touching the desktop. Ask your partner to put the textbook in your outstretched hand. Grasp the book firmly.

2. Raise the book toward your head. Count how many times you can touch the top of your head with the textbook in 30 seconds. Record your data.

3. Rest for 1 minute. Repeat with your right arm. Then, have your partner do the activity.

Number of lifts   Left arm _____   Right arm _____

 Answer these questions.

1. Study your data. Which of your arms had the better muscle tone?

_____

2. Make a hypothesis that explains any differences between the strength of your right and left arms.

_____

_____

3. What exercises could you do to strengthen the muscles of your arms?

_____

4. Would it be easier to improve muscle tone for voluntary muscles or involuntary muscles? Explain.

_____

_____

Reproduction and Heredity

All living things must **reproduce**, or make more living things like themselves. If a species did not reproduce, all living things of its kind would die out. The reproductive system of humans allows people to make more humans, or to have children.

When people have children, they pass on certain **traits** and characteristics. This is called **heredity**. Heredity affects the way you look and the way you act. You may have noticed that when adults look at a new baby, they often talk about which parent the baby looks like. This is because the baby has inherited its looks from its parents. As a child grows, there may be times when the child looks more like the mother, and times when the child looks more like the father. There will be certain things the child does that will remind people of the mother or the father, or even of some other relative. All these things are inherited. Other things, such as likes and dislikes and personal fitness, are not inherited. These are the result of the person's lifestyle and environment.

When you study cells, you learn that the nucleus of a cell contains **chromosomes**. On the chromosomes are **genes**. Genes determine how offspring will look and act. Each child receives genes from both parents, but some genes are stronger than others are. These genes are called dominant genes. The weaker genes are called recessive genes.

Here is an example. The gene for brown hair is a dominant gene. We say that brown hair is a dominant trait. Blond hair is a recessive trait. If both parents have brown hair, their children will probably have brown hair. If one parent has brown hair, and the other parent has blond hair, the children will still most likely have brown hair, but it is possible for a child to have blond hair. If both parents are blond, then the children will probably be blond.

The combinations can be seen in a chart like this. A brown-haired father may carry a blond-haired gene, but the brown-haired gene will dominate. He may pass on genes like this: Bb

A blond-haired mother cannot have a brown-haired gene. She must pass on genes like this: bb

To see what combinations of genes the children can receive, we can make a chart.

In this family, it is possible that half of the children could have blond hair, or there is a 50% chance that a child could have blond hair.

	B	b
b	Bb	bb
b	Bb	bb

GO ON TO THE NEXT PAGE ☞

Reproduction and Heredity, p. 2

◻ **If the father had not had a blond gene, he would have passed on genes like this: BB. Now what do the combinations look like? How many children can have blond hair now? Complete the chart.**

	B	B
b		
b		

There are sometimes exceptions to the rules, but they hold true most of the time. Look at your own family. Can you tell which traits, or characteristics, you received from each of your parents? Do you have the same mannerisms as your father or your mother?

◻ **Make a chart about your family. You may wish to consider other close relatives as well. What family resemblances do you see?**

Family Member	Hair Color	Eye Color	Height	Shape of Face	Mannerisms You Share

Sense Organs and the Brain

Your **nervous system** controls your reactions. In this activity, you and a partner will measure the time it takes for a person to react.

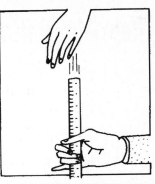

You will need

☆ meter stick   ☆ nontransparent tape, such as masking tape

1. Wrap the tape around the stick so that one piece is lined up with the 30 cm mark and the other with the 40 cm mark.

2. One partner should sit with his or her writing arm resting on a desk. The arm should extend beyond the edge of the desk to a point midway between the wrist and elbow.

3. The other partner should stand holding the meter stick at the 100 cm mark. The meter stick should hang within grasp of the seated partner at the 30 cm mark.

4. The seated partner should concentrate on the 40 cm tape mark and be ready to snap his or her fingers shut on that mark when the meter stick begins falling.

5. The standing partner should release the stick without warning. The seated partner should grab the stick. Measure how far the stick fell from the 30 cm mark.

6. Switch places and repeat the above steps.

7. What you measured was the reaction distance. To find the reaction time, use the table shown.

8. Record your results in the chart below.

DISTANCE OF FALL (cm)	TIME OF FALL (s)
1	0.045
2	0.064
3	0.078
4	0.090
5	0.101
6	0.110
7	0.120
8	0.128
9	0.136
10	0.143
11	0.150
12	0.157
13	0.163
14	0.169
15	0.175
16	0.181
17	0.186
18	0.192
19	0.197
20	0.202
21	0.207
22	0.212
23	0.217
24	0.221
25	0.226
26	0.230
27	0.235
28	0.239
29	0.243
30	0.247
31	0.252
32	0.256
33	0.259
34	0.263
35	0.267
36	0.271
37	0.275
38	0.279
39	0.282
40	0.286

	Distance	Time
You		
Partner		

 Answer these questions.

1. Who had the faster reaction time? _____

2. How did your senses and muscles work together in this activity? _____

_____

Your Sense of Smell

Your nose is the main sensory organ for your **sense of smell**. Your sense of smell allows you to recognize foods and other things by their **scent**.

📦 **Read the following paragraph. Then, number the sentences below the paragraph in the correct order.**

Arthur's father packed a surprise lunch for him today. Arthur thinks that his sandwich is peanut butter and jelly, as usual. When he sits down at the lunch table and opens his lunch bag, he will immediately know that his dad made him a tuna fish sandwich. How will Arthur know this?

_____ The message will be carried to Arthur's brain.

_____ Nerve cells in his nose will pick up the message of the odor of tuna fish.

_____ The message will be carried to his olfactory nerve.

_____ Air containing the odor of tuna fish will enter Arthur's nose.

_____ His brain will tell him that the sandwich smells like tuna fish.

📦 **Make a drawing that shows the parts of the body that provide you with a sense of smell. Label each part. Use a reference book if you need help.**

Name _____ Date _____

Your Sense of Taste

Your **sense of taste** is closely related to your sense of smell. The tongue is the main sensory organ for your sense of taste. There are four kinds of **taste buds** located on your tongue. These taste buds can identify four kinds of flavors: sweet, sour, salty, and bitter.

Below are some body parts that allow you to taste food. Arrange them in the order that shows how they are used as you taste something. Then, write the letters on the lines above each number. Leave a blank space between words. You will have more blanks than you need.

Body part	Correct order	Code words											
Brain		1	2	3	4	5	6	7	8	9	10	11	12
Taste buds		13	14	15	16	17	18	19	20	21	22	23	24
Taste nerves		25	26	27	28	29	30	31	32	33	34	35	36

A secret code word contains these coded letters: 28, 19, 33, 4, 13, 29.

Unscramble the letters for the secret code word:

_____

The drawing to the right shows an outline of a tongue. Draw in the places that show where each of the four tastes are detected. Label the name of each taste. Use a reference book if you need help.

Test Your Sense of Taste

How good is your sense of taste? Work with partners to find out.

You will need

- ☆ blindfold
- ☆ 10 toothpicks
- ☆ 2 paper cups of water
- ☆ 2 each of 5 food samples

(You may wish to use 10 different foods and keep the cups covered so that the tasters do not see the foods before they taste them.)

1. Prepare five food samples for each partner, each in a numbered cup.

2. Blindfold the taster.

3. Using a toothpick, pick up a small amount of one food sample. Tell the taster to hold his or her nose. Then, place the food on the taster's tongue.

4. Tell the taster to roll the sample around on his or her tongue. Then, ask the taster to identify the type of taste (sweet, bitter, salty, etc.) and to name the food. Record the response in your chart. Prepare a chart for each partner.

5. Repeat steps 3 and 4 with each food sample. Have the taster drink some water after each sample to clear the taste buds. Use a new toothpick each time.

6. Continue to test other people. Record the results.

Sample	Type of Taste	Type of Food

Answer these questions on another sheet of paper.

1. Were there any food samples that the tasters could not identify?
2. Which ones did each taster guess correctly?
3. Why might a taster have difficulty identifying some of the foods?
4. Would the results be the same if the tasters could see the food? Why or why not?
5. Would the results be the same if the tasters did not hold their noses? Why or why not?

Your Sense of Hearing

Your **sense of hearing** allows you to capture and identify sound waves. Your ear is your main sensory organ for hearing.

📦 **Pamela is listening to an orchestra. For her to hear the music, many things happen in her body. Below is a scrambled list of some of these events. Rewrite the events in order from the first thing that happens to the last.**

The vibrating eardrum passes the message to nearby bones.

The auditory nerve carries the message to the brain.

Sound vibrations caused by the instruments reach the eardrum.

Bones vibrate and pass the message to the auditory nerve.

_____

_____

_____

_____

_____

_____

_____

📦 **If you cup your hands behind your ears when you listen to a sound, do you think the sound will be louder or softer? Explain your answer.**

_____

_____

_____

_____

_____

Are Two Ears Better Than One?

You have two ears. Could you hear just as well with one ear? To find out, try this activity.

You will need

★ blindfold (A roll of white crepe-paper may be used to make disposable blindfolds.)

1. Work with a partner. Have your partner sit down and put on a blindfold.

2. At a distance of about 3 m from your partner, clap your hands. Ask your partner to point to where the sound came from. Do this 10 times from different locations. Record the number of right and wrong responses in your chart. Prepare a chart for each partner.

3. Have your partner press a cupped hand tightly over his or her right ear. Repeat step 2.

4. Now, have your partner uncover the right ear and press a cupped hand over the left ear. Repeat step 2.

5. Switch places with your partner and repeat the activity.

	Student 1		Student 2	
	Right	**Wrong**	**Right**	**Wrong**
Ears uncovered				
Right ear covered				
Left ear covered				

Answer these questions on another sheet of paper.

1. How many correct responses did you and your partner make with both ears uncovered?
2. How many did you make with the right ear covered?
3. How many did you make with the left ear covered?
4. Is it easier to locate the direction of a sound when listening with both ears or with just one ear? Explain your answer.

Your Sense of Sight

Your **sense of sight** allows you to receive light waves to see things. The eyes are the main sensory organs that produce **vision**. This exercise will help you learn about how you see.

Names of parts of your body that help you see are scrambled below. Unscramble each term and rewrite it in the space provided. You may use a science book or an encyclopedia if you need help.

1. SLEN   _____

2. SIIR   _____

3. POTIC REVEN   _____

4. TERANI   _____

5. PLIPU   _____

Select the term above that best fits each of these definitions.

_____ **6.** the nerve that carries sight messages to the brain

_____ **7.** the part of the eye that changes light into a pattern

_____ **8.** the opening in the center of your iris

_____ **9.** the colored part of the eye

_____ **10.** the back part of the eye where images are focused

Write two sentences that compare the pairs of terms below. Use a reference book if you need help.

11. farsightedness and nearsightedness

_____

_____

_____

12. the human eye and a camera

_____

_____

_____

How Does Light Affect the Pupils of Your Eyes?

Light must enter your eyes for you to see. The **pupils** control how much light enters the eyes. To find out how light affects the pupils, try this activity.

You will need

☆ a mirror

1. In normal light, look at your eyes in a mirror. Notice the size of the pupils.

2. Look at the chart of pupil sizes. Find the circle closest in size to your pupil. Circle the letter of the circle. Under it, write **Normal Light**.

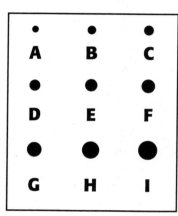

3. Your teacher will dim the lights in the classroom. Wait 10 seconds. Then, look again at your eyes in the mirror.

4. Circle the letter of the circle closest in size to your pupil now. Under it, write **Dim Light**.

5. Your teacher will turn the lights back on. After 10 seconds, look at your eyes again. Again, circle the letter of the circle closest in size to your pupils. Under it, write **Normal Light**.

 Answer these questions.

1. What happened to the size of your pupils when the lights were dimmed?

   _____

2. What happened when the lights were turned back on?

   _____

3. How do the pupils of your eyes react to light?

   _____

4. Use a reference book to find out why your pupils do this. What did you find out?

   _____

   _____

   _____

   _____

   _____

Seeing an Afterimage

The lens in your eye changes light into a pattern, or image, that is focused on the retina, or back of the eye. The optic nerve then transfers the image from the retina to the brain. When you look at an object quickly and then look away or shut your eyes, the image of the object remains for a short time, about $\frac{1}{16}$ of a second. For example, if you look at a candle and then move the candle away, you will see the candle for a short time after it was moved. Scientists call this an **afterimage**. In this activity, you will see an afterimage.

You will need

☆ index card   ☆ black marking pencil   ☆ tape

1. Draw a tree with branches on one side of the card.

2. Turn the card over and hold it up to the light. Draw dots on the blank side of the card where you see the tops of the branches.

3. Place the card on your desk and draw a bird at each dot.

4. Tape the card to the top of the pencil.

5. Roll the pencil back and forth quickly between your hands. As you do this, look at the card.

Answer these questions.

1. What did you see? Why?

_____

_____

_____

2. On what part of the eye is the image focused? _____

3. A piece of motion picture film is made of many different pictures, which are shown very rapidly. How does a film show motion? Use the word *afterimage* in your answer.

_____

_____

_____

Your Sense of Touch

Your **sense of touch** tells you when your body has made contact with another object. The sense of touch can tell you the shape and texture of an object, and it tells you about temperature, pain, and pressure.

Your skin is a sense organ. Within your skin are **nerve endings** that give you information about touch. There are more nerve endings, or **receptors** to touch, in some parts of the body than there are in others. Some receptors are deeper in the skin than others. If you touch your skin lightly, you feel touch. If you add pressure, you will stimulate the receptors deeper in the skin. Then, you will feel pain.

There are many receptors in the skin. Each receptor senses only one kind of message. The information is carried by the nerve cells to the spinal cord, and then to the brain. The brain sends signals to the body that tell it what to do.

Answer these questions.

1. Your body has five types of sense receptors. Can you write the names of all of them? Use a reference book if you need help.

   a. _____ b. _____ c. _____

   d. _____ e. _____

2. Look at the drawing. Label the brain, spinal cord, and nerves.

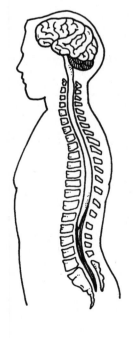
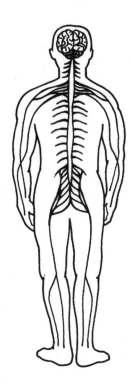

How Does Skin Protect Against Infection?

Bright and shiny apples—red, green, and yellow. The "skin" of an apple is more than just something colorful to look at. Find out how skin is helpful in this activity.

You will need

⭐ 2 fresh apples

⭐ 1 rotten apple

⭐ 2 small paper plates

⭐ crayon or marking pen

⭐ plastic knife

1. Label one of the paper plates **uncut skin**. Label the other one **cut skin**.

2. Place a fresh apple on each paper plate.

3. Cut a badly spoiled piece off the rotten apple.

4. Cut a small piece of skin off the apple labeled cut skin. Rub the piece of the rotten apple on the area where the skin has been removed. Some of the rotten apple should stick to the fresh apple.

5. Next, rub the same place of the rotten apple on the apple labeled uncut skin.

6. Throw away the small pieces of the apple and the rest of the rotten apple. Clean up your area and wash your hands.

7. Put the paper plates with the apples aside. Observe the cut and the uncut apples each day for one week. Take notes on your observations each day.

🔲 **Answer these questions.**

1. Describe what happened to the cut and uncut apples. How can you explain a difference in the two apples?

_____

_____

_____

2. How is your skin like the skin of an apple?

_____

_____

Good Hygiene

An important part of staying healthy is keeping your teeth and your body clean. It is important to keep the germs and bacteria that can come in contact with your body from spreading. This is why you wash your body and hair. It is very important that you wash your hands whenever you handle garbage or raw meats (such as when you make a hamburger) and each time you use the bathroom. Germs can be spread easily from person to person, too. If you cough or sneeze without covering your mouth, germs fly out into the air and onto other people. If you cover your mouth, the germs are contained, and it is less likely that you will spread your germs to someone else. It is not a good idea to share straws, cups, combs, or hats, either. Germs can be passed from one person to the next this way, as well.

Brushing your teeth keeps bacteria from living in your mouth. Bacteria eat small particles of food that are in your mouth. Acids can form that eat into the enamel that protects your teeth. When acid eats into your teeth, decay begins, and you will get cavities. So it is important that you brush your teeth after every meal. Just brushing is not enough, however. If you do not floss, you cannot get all the small food particles from between your teeth, and bacteria will grow anyway. If you get gum disease, the gums will not be able to hold your teeth in place, and they will fall out. Visits to the dentist can help keep your teeth strong and healthy, too. The dentist can see problems with X-rays that can be missed otherwise. Then, the dentist can take preventive measures to help your teeth. Brushing, flossing, and visiting the dentist regularly will keep your teeth and gums healthy for many years to come.

Good **hygiene** helps to keep you healthy and feeling good. It makes you look and smell better, too! Do you have good hygiene habits?

Answer the following questions to see if you need to improve your hygiene.

	Yes	No
1. Do you take a bath or shower every day?	_____	_____
2. Do you brush your teeth at least twice a day?	_____	_____
3. Do you floss your teeth every day?	_____	_____
4. Do you visit the dentist regularly?	_____	_____
5. Do you cover your mouth when you sneeze or cough?	_____	_____
6. Do you wash your hands after using the bathroom?	_____	_____
7. Do you wash your hands after handling garbage or raw meats?	_____	_____
8. Do you share combs, hats, or other items that go in the hair?	_____	_____
9. Do you share cups, straws, or other eating utensils?	_____	_____

If you answered yes to 1–7, and no to 8 and 9, good for you! You have good hygiene habits already! If not, try to improve your habits, and take the test again in two weeks!

Science Grade 5
Answer Key

Pages 4–6
1. T, **2.** T, **3.** T, **4.** F, **5.** F, **6.** T, **7.** B, **8.** B, **9.** D,
10. B, **11.** A, **12.** A, **13.** T, **14.** T, **15.** T, **16.** T,
17. T, **18.** T, **19.** B, **20.** C, **21.** C, **22.** B, **23.** D,
24. C, **25.** b, **26.** f, **27.** e, **28.** c, **29.** d, **30.** a,
31. carbon dioxide, **32.** amphibians,
33. vertebrates, **34.** Photosynthesis,
35. mammals, **36.** gymnosperms

Pages 13–14
1. F, **2.** F, **3.** T, **4.** T, **5.** T, **6.** T, **7.** T, **8.** F, **9.** A,
10. D, **11.** D, **12.** B, **13.** C, **14.** D, **15.** A, **16.** A,
17. A, **18.** A, **19.** C, **20.** B

Page 15
1. C, **2.** B, **3.** D, **4.** A

Page 16
1. Matter is anything that has volume and mass;
gases, liquids, and solids are all made up of
matter., **2.** Answers will vary. Possible response:
solid; round shape; about 3 inches in diameter;
orange-yellow color; sweet or tart taste; smooth,
bumpy texture on the outside; juicy on the
inside., **3.** Answers will vary. Possible response:
Standard units are always the same and do not
change; if standard units are used, anyone can
make the same measurements and get the same
results; measurements will not be accurate if
standard units are not used.

Page 17
1. a. gas, b. solid, c. liquid, **2.** Water drops form on
a glass containing a cold drink because the water
vapor (gas) in the air is cooled when it touches the
cold glass. It causes the water to change to its
liquid phase., **3.** Water is in its liquid state and
changes to water vapor when heat is added.

Page 18
1. gas, **2.** liquid, **3.** solid, **4.** gas, **5.** solid,
6. Molecules in a liquid slide over each other and
move faster than molecules in a solid, which are
packed tightly and only vibrate.

Pages 19–20
1. Possible response: Heat is a form of energy. As
an object becomes hotter, its atoms and molecules
move faster. Temperature is the measure of the
average kinetic energy, or energy of movement, of
the atoms and molecules in a substance or an
object., **2.** Possible response: When a solid, liquid,
or gas is heated, the molecules begin to move
faster, and they expand and take up more room.,
3. gas, liquid, solid, **4.** Possible response: This
form of heat movement occurs when atoms or
molecules bump into one another and heat energy
is transferred from one atom or molecule to
another through contact. Solids, liquids, and gases
can all be heated by this form of heat movement.,
5. Possible response: This form of heat movement
occurs when heat energy is transferred by currents
of molecules in liquids and gases. As molecules
become hotter, they move faster and spread out.
The warmer molecules are pushed up by the
cooler, more dense molecules and produce
currents., **6.** Possible response: This form of heat
movement occurs without the movement of any
molecules. Instead, the heat is transferred by
radiation, or by infrared rays. These rays travel in
straight lines as fast as light. The Sun's rays travel
through space to Earth and produce radiant heat.,
7. C, **8.** A

Page 21
1. If the balance is weighted in one direction,
the measurement of mass will not be accurate.,
2. Find the sum of the gram weights.,
3. Answers will vary.

Page 22
1. Ruler; The sides of the tank are straight.,
2. Water in a measuring cup; The keys have an
irregular shape that cannot be measured with a
ruler., **3.** Answers will vary.

Page 23
1. Answers will vary., **2.** Answers will vary.,
3. 100 g, **4.** 100 g divided by 100 mL = 1 g/mL,
Chart: Answers will vary.

Page 24
1. A chemical change produces a new chemical.
A physical change changes only the appearance
or state., **2.** A new substance forms, the color
changes, heat or light is given off, or bubbles
form., **3.** physical change, chemical change

Page 25
1. C, **2.** B, **3.** A, **4.** D, **5.** The solvent is the
material in which the solute is dissolved. The
solute is the material that dissolves in the
solvent. In lemonade, water is the solvent and the
lemonade mix is the solute.

Page 26
1. Mixtures are made by a physical change and
can be separated back into their individual parts.
Compounds are formed by a chemical change.,
2. Water is formed when 2 atoms of hydrogen
gas combine with 1 atom of oxygen gas and
become clear liquid water.

Page 27
1. Carbon and oxygen become carbon dioxide.,
2. Hydrogen and oxygen become water.,
3. Mercuric oxide becomes mercury and
oxygen., **4.** Iron sulfide becomes iron and sulfur.,
5. calcium, **6.** zinc

Page 28
Step 2: The popcorn sinks.; It is more dense than
water., Step 3: Bubbles form.; They rise to the
surface.; It is less dense than water., Step 4:
Bubbles should begin to collect on the popcorn.
The bubbles should float the popcorn to the top
of the jar. Bubbles of carbon dioxide break off
when the popcorn reaches the surface and the
popcorn sinks. As more carbon dioxide bubbles
collect, the popcorn rises again. Carbon dioxide
can carry a substance that is denser than water to
the water's surface.

Page 29
Answers will vary depending on the colors used.

Page 30
milk-neutral; lemon juice-acid; dish soap-base;
sugar water-neutral; carbonated drink-acid

Page 31
1. The balloon expanded due to the carbon dioxide
gas., **2.** yes, **3.** Yes; The weight of the substances
was exactly the same before and after the chemical
reaction.

Page 32
1. Arrows face in and begin at each wrestler's
shoulders.; **2.** push; **3.** push or pull; **4.** push or pull;
5. pull; **6.** push or pull; **7.** pull; **8.** push; **9.** pull

Page 33
1. It moved backward, in a direction away from the
carton., **2.** It moved forward, in the opposite
direction of the air., **3.** The air coming out of the
balloon was the action force., **4.** The forward
movement of the carton was the reaction force.,
5. Newton's third law of motion states that for
every action, there is an equal and opposite
reaction., **6.** A propeller pushes backward against
the water, like the air flowing from the balloon.
The water pushes forward just as it did in the
experiment.

Page 34
1. They hit the ground at the same time.,
2. The force of gravity varies according to mass.
The force of gravity increases as the mass
increases so that it makes them fall at the same
time., **3.** A force is a push or pull. Gravity is a
pull that draws all objects toward the center of
the Earth.

Page 35
1. Earth; The largest force is required to lift
the objects on Earth., **2.** Planet Y; The least amount
of force is required on planet Y., **3.** Earth's gravity
= 5 x planet Y's gravity, **4.** Earth's gravity = 2.5 x
planet X's gravity, **5.** Planet X's gravity = 2 x
planet Y's gravity, **6.** Object 5 requires the greatest
force to lift it., **7.** 5, 1, 3, 2, 4, **8.** Object 1 has 4
times the mass of object 4.

Page 36
1. gravity, **2.** collision of 2 objects, **3.** The string
keeps the ball in circular motion until it is cut,
then the ball travels in a straight path.

Page 37
1. The forces were the force caused by squeezing
the bottle, which made the cup move up, and
gravity, which pulled it downward., **2.** The
downward force of gravity was not as strong as
the upward force of the plug., **3.** No; balanced
forces do not cause movement.

Page 38
1. C, **2.** D, **3.** A, **4.** B

Page 39
1. The walls and other objects in the room
appear to move., **2.** The pencil is the frame of
reference., **3.** The pencil appears to move.,
4. The walls and other objects are the frame of
reference.

Page 40
1. Answers will vary., **2.** Answers will vary.,
3. Since the speed for any one trial may be
atypical, finding the average speed for several
trials lessens the possibility of an inaccurate
measurement., **4.** Answers will vary. Possible
responses: amount of time it took the marble to
reach the tape; friction.

Page 42
1. 64 - 48 = 16 km/hr (10 mi/hr) east,
2. The difference in velocity tells how fast the
faster vehicle is pulling away from the slower
one., **3.** Relative velocities could be used to
calculate how much sooner one vehicle would
arrive at a certain location or how long it would
take one vehicle to overtake the other., **4.** 56 +
40 = 96 km/hr (60 mi/hr), **5.** 1,012 km/hr (629
mi/hr) east

Page 43

1. B, 2. A, 3. B, 4. C, 5. A, 6. C

Page 45

1. Answers will vary., 2. Answers will vary, but the number of vibrations should be less for the rock than the washer., 3. It was easier to move the washer. Since the washer had less mass, less force was needed to move it., 4. The rock had greater inertia since it had more mass., 5. The rock had greater mass because it was made up of more matter.

Page 46

1. Moving the bottle forward made the bubble move forward. Moving it backwards made the bubble move backwards. A left turn made the bubble move left, too., 2. Velocity changes when direction changes. Acceleration is the rate of change in velocity.

Page 47

1. pennies, 2. Answers will vary. The distance between each drop of water and the next is a measure of acceleration and should have increased as the truck progressed., 3. Answers will vary. Distance was greater between those water drops falling from the truck without sand than between those falling from the truck carrying sand., 4. The truck without the sand accelerated faster, because the distance between the drops of water was greater., 5. When the sand was removed, the truck's mass was decreased and its acceleration increased.

Page 48

1. A, 2. B, 3. D, 4. B

Page 49

1. A, 2. D, 3. B

Page 50

The bulb should light up.

Page 52

1. aluminum foil, door key, penny, 2. paper, rubber band, pencil, 3. Answers will vary., 4. Metals make good conductors.

Page 53

1. Both light bulbs were lit, 2. None of the light bulbs was lit., 3. An electric current can flow through only one path in a series circuit. When one light bulb was unscrewed, the electric current could not flow through the circuit., 4. If one light bulb in a series circuit is not in its socket, then the other light bulbs will not light. If all the light bulbs in a series circuit are in their sockets, then the entire circuit will light.

Page 54

1. All the bulbs were lit., 2. All the bulbs were lit except the one unscrewed., 3. An electric current can flow through as many paths as there are wires. Each object has two wires that keep the current moving. Even if one light bulb is unscrewed, the others remain lit because there are other paths for the current to travel., 4. A parallel circuit has more than one path for charges. A series circuit has only one path.

Page 55

For 2.–4., drawings may vary.

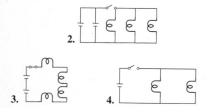

Page 56

1. Touching the bare wires with the screwdriver caused the circuit to short., 2. The current traveled through the screwdriver., 3. The foil melted. The current got too hot and heated the foil., 4. A fuse can stop the surge of current from damaging the wires and appliances.

Page 57

1. The nails were magnetized when they were rubbed in one direction with the magnet., 2. The nails lost their magnetism., 3. The nail lost its magnetism., 4. Heating, hammering, or rubbing the nail with a magnet in both directions will destroy magnetism.

Page 58

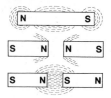

4. *N* stands for north; *S* stands for south.
5. Answers will vary

Page 59

1. The space around a magnet is a magnetic field., 2. The poles of a magnet have the strongest magnetic field.

Page 60

1. The paper clip is held by the magnetic field., 2. Nothing happened because paper does not interfere with a magnetic field., 3. The iron nail did, because it is made of a material attracted by a magnet., 4. There was no difference because the poles react the same to metal and nonmetal objects.

Page 61

1. c, a, b, d, 2. Check students' work.

Pages 69–70

1. F, 2. T, 3. F, 4. F, 5. F, 6. T, 7. T, 8. T, 9. A, 10. D, 11. B, 12. A, 13. C, 14. B, 15. B, 16. B, 17. A, 18. D, 19. C, 20. B

Page 71

1. mantle, core, 2. seismograph, 3. Students should label the diagram correctly with these parts: outer core, inner core, crust, upper mantle, lower mantle, 4. Rock of the oceanic crust is heavier than rock of the continental crust. Rock under the continents is thicker than rock under the oceans., 5. Upper-mantle rocks are hard, whereas lower-mantle rocks are soft., 6. The outer core is liquid, whereas the inner core is solid.

Page 72

1. B, 2. C, 3. A, 4. A, 5. Igneous rocks are formed from melted rock that cools inside or outside the Earth's surface. Metamorphic rocks are formed from other rocks that are exposed to heat and pressure beneath the Earth's surface.

Page 73

1. F, 2. T, 3. T, 4. F, 5. T, 6. Soil is made up of mineral material and humus. The mineral material comes from rock that has been broken up in many ways. Rock can be broken up by moving water or by wind. Once the rock is broken up, it is mixed with humus, or decayed pieces of once-living plants and animals.

Page 74

1. T, 2. F, 3. F, 4. T, 5. A, 6. B

Page 75

1. Soil is formed from parent material that is on or near the Earth's surface. The parent material is broken into small pieces in a process called weathering. Plants begin growing in the rock pieces, and insects move in. When these plants

and insects die, they break down and become part of the soil., 2. to keep the soil from blowing away, 3. To keep the soil from eroding, farmers can plant cover crops when the growing season is over. Farmers can also plant crops across hills rather than up and down them.

Page 76

1. "all Earth", 2. the existence of the fossil Mesosaurus in both South America and Africa, 3. The plates float and move on the semisolid lower mantle., 4. The Earth's crust is broken into about 10 pieces, just as a jigsaw puzzle has pieces. At one time, all the continent plates fit together into one large land mass, like the picture the jigsaw puzzle makes.

Page 77

Answers will vary, but students should notice that the continents fit together fairly well.; Paragraphs will vary.

Page 78

1. B, 2. A, 3. A, 4. C, 5. C, 6. C

Page 79

1. Arrows point at each other; mountains form., Arrows point in opposite directions; volcanoes or earthquakes occur., Arrows point in opposite directions diagonally; earthquakes occur., 2. The plates can push against each other, or collide; move apart, or spread; slide past each other, or slip.

Page 81

1. One rock wall could drop down, leaving the other rock wall higher. A normal fault could help form a mountain like this., 2. A normal fault forms when rock walls pull away from each other. A reverse fault forms when rock walls push against each other., 3. If this curb were on a fault line, a lateral fault could pull it apart like this., 4. Answers will vary, but this is probably not a good idea because of the potential for earthquakes and damage near faults.

Page 82

1. Students should label magma inside and below volcano; lava outside volcano., 2. Correct order: 6, 1, 5, 3, 4, 7, 2

Page 83

Correct order: 1, 5, 3, 2, 4

Page 84

1. The newest rocks are on the top and the oldest are on the bottom., 2. Both rock layers and landfills are laid down in layers. By examining the layers, you can discover information about the history of the land or the landfill. The difference is that landfills are recent, and rock layers may have been there for millions of years., 3. Scientists know when many organisms lived on the Earth. The organisms would be embedded in a rock layer of the same age., 4. The mountain must have been under water at some time.

Page 85

1. B, 2. C, 3. C, 4. A, 5. B, 6. A, 7. B

Page 86

1. Gravity pulls weathered rock and soil down hills. Erosion by gravity can cause landslides or rockslides., 2. Weathering is the process by which rock is broken down into small pieces. Erosion is the movement of those pieces by water, wind, and gravity., 3. Glaciers change the land when they carve out huge bowl-shaped hollows called cirques. As the glaciers move, they scrape the land they pass over, leaving long U-shaped valleys., 4. Rivers erode the land by washing away parts of it. They may cut into the land and leave deep canyons. Glaciers cause erosion by dragging ice and debris over the land, scraping it and making it flat.

Page 87
1. Yes; in the cross section, you can see that a mesa has a flat top like a table and rises above the surrounding area like a table above a floor., **2.** 2,200 m; 2,000 m; 1,500 m, **3.** Layer B is softer. Layer B is worn away more than layer A, even though layer A is above it. Softer rock is worn away more quickly than harder rock., **4.** D would be in danger, but not C. From the cross section, you can see that point D is at the same elevation as the river's bank and so could be under 7 meters of water. The elevation scale shows that point C is about 100 meters above the river's bank and would not be reached by the rising water.

Page 88
1. Yes; The needle's direction can be judged by other known directions, such as east and west., **2.** No; the moon has almost no magnetic field.

Page 89
1. It feels much cooler., **2.** It evaporates., **3.** The temperature seems to lower., **4.** Answers will vary but should indicate the surface becomes cooler.

Page 91
1. Answers will vary but should be similar., **2.** Predictions will vary. Have students repeat the readings outside the classroom and compare their first and second readings., **3.** Students should predict that relative humidity will be higher. Have students repeat the experiment on the next rainy or damp day when the temperature is about the same as when they first did the experiment. The relative humidity reading should be higher.

Page 92
1. D, **2.** C, **3.** Possible responses: You cannot drink salt water; salt water freezes more slowly than fresh water; things float better in salt water than they do in fresh water.

Page 93
Graphs should reflect data in the charts.;
1. Pacific, **2.** Indian, **3.** Atlantic

Page 94
Top: 1, 5, 2, 6, 3, Bottom: 4

Page 95
1. A, **2.** C, **3.** Answers should use information from the chart.

Page 96
1. the thermometer at the bottom, **2.** The cold water from the ice cube sank, and warm water rose to replace the cold water., **3.** Cold water and warm water moving between the poles and the Equator cause ocean currents.

Page 97
2. yes, **4.** Cup 2; It contains more salt.; Cup 2, **6.** The blue water sinks.; It is denser than the red water., **7.** the bottom, **8.** As denser water sinks below less dense water, it can cause a current to form.

Page 98
1. The gentle waves carried some sand away from the beach., **2.** The storm waves carried greater quantities of sand away from the beach., **3.** Sand was moved into the water., **4.** Waves are constantly reshaping the beaches along the shoreline.

Page 100
1. There are two low tides each day., **2.** about 12 hours elapse, **3.** Wednesday: 12 hr 16 min, 12 hr 41 min; Thursday: 12 hr 20 min, 12 hr 34 min; Friday: 12 hr 17 min, 12 hr 29 min; Saturday: 12 hr 25 min, 12 hr 27 min; Sunday: 12 hr 22 min, 12 hr 26 min; Monday: 12 hr 18 min, 12 hr 26 min, **4.** 54 minutes, **5.** 49 minutes

Page 101
1. Layers should be, from top: plain water, salty water, very salty water, **2.** It is heavier than plain water., **3.** The ocean water, which is salty, would be on the bottom.

Page 102
Students should label diagram, from top: exosphere, ionosphere, stratosphere, troposphere.

Page 103
1. First, Earth's land and water are warmed by the Sun's energy, which causes air masses of different densities, which causes wind. Second, the Sun warms the Earth's surface, causing the stages of the water cycle., **2.** The movement of air from where it is dense to where it is less dense., **3.** On a summer day, land heats faster than water, causing the air over the land to become less dense. The wind blows toward the land. On a summer night, the water stays warm longer than the land, so the air over the water is less dense and the wind blows toward the sea. Air moves from areas where it is dense to areas where it is less dense., **4.** cirrus, stratus, cumulus, **5.** As warm, moist air rises, it cools, and the moisture condenses, forming clouds.

Page 104
1. An air mass has about the same temperature, pressure, and humidity throughout., **2.** Air over land will be drier., **3.** Air over water will be moist., **4.** warm, cold, stationary, **5.** Answers will vary.

Page 105
1. B, **2.** B, **3.** C, **4.** Tornadoes are small but very intense storms that form from low-pressure areas along a line of severe thunderstorms called a squall line. Tornadoes are characterized by funnels that dip down from the clouds. The extremely high winds, which cause almost total destruction, are the most notable feature of tornadoes., **5.** Answers will vary.

Page 106
1. tropical, **2.** polar, **3.** temperate, **4.** Answers will vary., **5.** Drawings will vary.

Page 107
Students should label the diagram correctly; from center: Sun, Mercury, Venus, Earth, Mars, asteroids, Jupiter, Saturn, Uranus, Neptune, Pluto

Page 108
1. The inner planets are about evenly spaced and are close together. The distances keep doubling for the outer planets., **2.** between Mars and Jupiter, **3.** from beyond Pluto toward the Sun

Page 109
Students should label diagram as follows: top, spring equinox; right, winter solstice; bottom, fall equinox; left, summer solstice.

Page 110
1. 29.5 x 12 = 354 days, **2.** 365 - 354 = 11 days, **3.** Step 1: Multiply 28 x 365 to find the number of solar days. Step 2: Add 7 days to account for leap year. Step 3: Divide the result by 354.; 28.89 yrs.

Page 111
1. inside the tennis ball, but not its center, **2.** inside the tennis ball; under the balance point, **3.** yes

Page 112
1. B, **2.** C, **3.** B, **4.** C

Page 113
1. nebula, **2.** yellow star, **3.** red giant, **4.** black dwarf.

Page 114
1. yellow, **2.** bluish-white, **3.** 10,000–8,000 degrees C, **4.** Aldebaran, **5.** Sirius, **6.** reddish, **7.** no, **8.** by spectrum and by temperature

Page 115
1. because scientists believe the formation of our universe began with a giant explosion., **2.** Milky Way, **3.** Barnard's star seems to wobble in its orbit. **4.** This motion could be caused by the pull of one or more planets orbiting it., **5.** Answers will vary.

Page 116
1. 4, **2.** 3, **3.** reflecting, **4.** 6, **5.** 8, **6.** Answers will vary.

Page 123
1. b, **2.** c, **3.** a, **4.** f, **5.** d, **6.** e, **7.** bones, **8.** food chain, **9.** cold-blooded, **10.** invertebrates, **11.** warm-blooded, **12.** arthropods

Page 124
1. cell, **2.** tissue, **3.** organ, **4.** system, **5.** systems, **6.** nervous, **7.** senses, **8.** brain, **9.** bones, **10.** muscles, **11.** joints, **12.** exercise, **13.** toned, **14.** blood, **15.** involuntary, **16.** voluntary, **17.** circulatory, **18.** respiratory, **19.** lungs, **20.** carbon dioxide, **21.** Red, **22.** White, **23.** hygiene, **24.** brushing, **25.** flossing, **26.** germs

Page 125
Diagram: a. cell membrane, b. mitochondria or organelle, c. nucleus, d. cytoplasm; **1.** Robert Hooke, **2.** cork, **3.** a. All plants and animals are made of cells., b. The cell is the basic unit of structure and function in all living things., c. Every cell can reproduce to form new cells.

Page 126
Pictures: cell membrane: b, f; cytoplasm: e, h; cell wall: a; chloroplasts: c; nucleus: d, g; **1.** cell wall, chloroplasts, **2.** chloroplasts, **3.** cell wall, **4.** cell membrane, **5.** cell a

Page 127
1. diffusion, **2.** dehydration, **3.** osmosis, **4.** organelles, **5.** chromosomes, **6.** The water that you lose when you sweat comes from the cells of your body. If that water is not replaced by drinking, your cells can become dehydrated. Dehydration can make you very sick, so you should always drink a lot when you sweat a lot., **7.** The cells of a wilted plant are dehydrated, just as your body cells are dehydrated when you sweat a lot. Watering a wilted plant is similar to your drinking a lot of water after sweating. The cells of the plant receive water from the soil by the process of osmosis.

Page 128
1. arctic tundra, **2.** deciduous forests, **3.** deserts, **4.** boreal forests, **5.** grasslands, **6.** tropical rain forests

Page 129
1. 50 cm; 25 cm; 400 cm; 75 cm; 50 cm; 25 cm, **2.** tropical rain forest; desert and arctic tundra, **3.** deciduous forest, **4.** plants and animals that require little water, such as cacti, rattlesnakes, scorpions, jackrabbits

Page 130
1. Animals breathe in oxygen., **2.** Animals breathe out carbon dioxide., **3.** Plants take in carbon dioxide., **4.** Plants use carbon dioxide, water, sunlight, and their own chlorophyll to make food., **5.** Plants give off oxygen.; Diagrams will vary, but should include the steps in questions 1–5.

Page 131
1. a gymnosperm, **2.** by seeds in cones, **3.** angiosperms, **4.** a tiny plant and stored food to help it grow, **5.** the seed for a fern or moss

Page 132

1. fat, rounded, filled out; firm, solid, **4.** flattened, wrinkled; soft; Roots and stems grew.; inside the bean, **5.** No roots or stems have grown from this bean.

Page 133

1. herring (or smaller fish), **2.** shark, **3.** the Sun, **4.** plant plankton, **5.** Animal plankton would have nothing to eat, so herrings would have nothing to eat, and so on. All the organisms in this food chain would eventually die.

Page 134

Invertebrates: starfish, sponge, beetle, spider, lobster, worm, ant, crab, snail, jellyfish, bee, shrimp; Vertebrates: mouse, turtle, fish, frog, lizard, bear, horse, eagle, rabbit, snake, human, dog

Page 135

Posters will vary.

Page 136

The pictures, clockwise from the top left and ending with the divided circle in the middle should be numbered: 1, 5, 3, 7, 4, 6, 2.

Page 137

1. cold blooded, **2.** It laid eggs., **3.** thick, scaly skin, **4.** It had thick skin that kept its body from drying out.; Comparison: Pteranodon: cold-blooded reptile with scaly skin, hollow bones and wings for flying; laid eggs. Condor: warm-blooded bird with feathers, hollow bones, and wings for flying; lays eggs.

Page 138

1. c, **2.** e, **3.** d, **4.** a, **5.** b

Page 139

1. The chimpanzee has eyes that face forward. The mouse has eyes that are at the sides of its head., **2.** The mouse, because it has chisel-like teeth., **3.** The chimpanzee, because it has well-developed hands., **4.** rodents, **5.** primates; Check students' graphs.

Page 140

Check students' diagrams.

Page 141

Answers will vary.

Page 142

1. The strip of newspaper in the container with the damp soil decomposed the most. Decomposers in the soil broke down the paper., **2.** The strips of newspaper in the dry containers remained dry. Decomposers need moisture in order to function., **3.** Decomposers were not present in the sand., **4.** They break down materials that would otherwise bury the Earth in waste; they release nutrients back into the food web., **5.** Arrows from plants to herbivores and omnivores; Arrows from herbivores to decomposers, scavengers, carnivores, and omnivores; Arrows from omnivores to decomposers, carnivores, and scavengers; Arrows from carnivores to omnivores, decomposers, and scavengers; Arrows from scavengers to decomposers, carnivores, and omnivores; Arrows from decomposers to plants.

Page 143

Reports will vary.

Page 144

Illustration: Responses will vary but should include buildings, roads, crops, animals, plants, and trash.; **1.** chemical fertilizers, acid rain, landfills, vehicle exhaust, **2. a.** reuse and recycle materials; **b.** use fewer chemical fertilizers and pesticides; **c.** use materials that can be broken down by organisms in soil and water, **3.** Recycling is important because it helps control pollution. It also saves natural resources, energy, and land.

Page 146

1. Possible responses: People need to get into the habit of recycling; some communities are not set up for recycling; some people may not know or may not care about the benefits of recycling., **2.** Possible responses: recycle; not litter; clean up parks or stretches of highway.

Page 147

1. stomach, organ; **2.** blood, tissue; **3.** leaf, organ; **4.** digestive, system; **5.** nerve, tissue; **6.** tree bark, tissue; **7.** muscle, tissue; **8.** lung, organ; **9.** oak tree, organism; **10.** nervous, system; **11.** liver, organ; **12.** amoeba, cell; **13.** cat, organism; **14.** circulatory, system

Page 148

1. c, **2.** b, **3.** a, **4.** f, **5.** e, **6.** d, **7.** Answers will vary.

Page 149

1. Answers will vary. Possible answers include: starchy., **2.** It should taste sweet.; An enzyme in saliva has changed some of the starch to sugar., **3.** Chew them. If they contain starch, they will begin to taste sweet after a bit., **4.** Results will vary.

Page 150

2. no, **5.** the cinnamon, **6.** salty; salt and water, **7.** It must be digested.

Page 151

1. d, **2.** a, **3.** f, **4.** h, **5.** b, **6.** g, **7.** e, **8.** c

Page 152

1. heart, **2.** artery, **3.** capillaries, **4.** vein, **5.** lungs; Match: 3, 5, 2, 1, 4

Page 153

1. false, **2.** true, **3.** true, **4.** false, **5.** true, **6.** false, **7.** false, **8.** true, **9.** true, **10.** true

Page 154

Across: **4.** respiratory, **6.** lungs, **7.** windpipe, **8.** nose; Down: **1.** diaphragm, **2.** bronchial, **3.** diffusion, **5.** sac

Page 155

1. Responses will vary but may include the fact that respiration rate increases with activity., **2.** The respiration rate increases.

Page 156

1. hinge, **2.** ball and socket; **3.–4.** Reports will vary.

Page 157

1. d, **2.** g, **3.** c, **4.** e, **5.** f, **6.** a, **7.** b

Page 158

1. Answers will vary., **2.** One arm is used more than the other. The more exercise the muscles get, the better the muscle tone., **3.** pushups, weight lifting, etc., **4.** It would be easier to improve the tone of your voluntary muscles because you can exercise them.

Page 160

Chart: Bb, Bb, Bb, Bb; None of the children is likely to have blond hair.

Page 161

1. Answers will vary. **2.** Your eye signaled your brain, which told your body when to react.

Page 162

Correct order: 4, 2, 3, 1, 5; Drawings should include brain, olfactory nerve, and nose.

Page 163

Order: Taste buds, Taste nerves, brain; Secret code word: bitter; Tongue: Top (back of tongue) should be labeled bitter, sides sour, near front is salty, and front is sweet.

Page 164

1. Answers will vary., **2.** Answers will vary., **3.** By holding the nostrils closed, the taster's sense of smell was not involved in the identification process. The sense of taste is affected by the sense of smell., **4.** The results would probably be different if the tasters had been able to see the food. After seeing the food, the tasters would probably decide what it tasted like before actually tasting the food sample., **5.** It is likely that the results would be different if the tasters did not hold their noses since odor information would be permitted to reach the brain.

Page 165

Order: Sound vibrations caused by the instruments reach the eardrum. The vibrating eardrum passes the message to nearby bones. Bones vibrate and pass the message to the auditory nerve. The auditory nerve carries the message to the brain.; Cupped ears: Louder, More sound vibrations would be funneled toward the eardrum.

Page 166

1. Answers will vary., **2–3.** Answers will vary, but probably fewer correct responses were made when either one or the other ear was covered., **4.** It is easier to locate the direction of a sound with both ears. Two ears, rather than one, enable humans to better judge the direction that sounds come from.

Page 167

1. lens, **2.** iris, **3.** optic nerve, **4.** retina, **5.** pupil, **6.** optic nerve, **7.** lens, **8.** pupil, **9.** iris, **10.** retina, **11.** A nearsighted person has trouble seeing objects that are far away. A farsighted person has trouble seeing objects that are nearby., **12.** The eye and the camera both have lenses and openings that allow in light. The image of an object is focused on the retina of the eye. The image is focused on the film in a camera.

Page 168

1. The size of the pupils was larger in the dim light., **2.** The pupils returned to their normal size., **3.** The pupils adjust to the amount of light in a room, growing smaller in bright light and larger in dim light., **4.** Answers will vary. Too much light in the eye can damage the eye. Not enough light impairs vision.

Page 169

1. The birds seemed to be on the branches. The image of the tree remained after the card was turned. The drawing of the birds appeared on the afterimage of the tree., **2.** retina, **3.** The image from each picture is formed on the retina. The afterimages of many pictures blend together. The images appear to be moving.

Page 170

1. In any order: a. sight, b. smell, c. taste, d. touch, e. hearing, **2.** Check students' labeling.

Page 171

1. The cut apple decayed quickly. The uncut apple stayed fresh, or started to decay only after several days. The skin of the uncut apple protected the apple from bacteria that were transferred from the rotten apple., **2.** The skin on the apple and the skin on a person's body give some protection from disease.